Praise for *Online Book Marketing*

So you've written a book! That's great, but your work is only half done. To make it successful, you need to spend as much time marketing your book as you did writing it. Fortunately, Lorraine Phillips shows you exactly what you need to do to build an online platform that delivers the results that you and your book deserve.

–David Meerman Scott, best-selling author of *The New Rules of Marketing and PR*, a *BusinessWeek* best seller published in more than 25 languages

Online Book Marketing is a comprehensive, resource-filled guide for anyone considering writing a book–whether for trade publishing or self-publishing. From cover to cover, it's a tightly organized, resource-filled, usable guide to author-driven book marketing a book in today's online world.

–Roger C. Parker, author of *#Book Title Tweet: 140 Bite-Sized Ideas for Article, Book, and Event Titles* (publishedandprofitable.com)

Lorraine Phillips is not only a master at clear explanations of highly technical concepts, but she has filled her book with hundreds of useful URLs: a wonderful tool kit for anyone wanting to market a book online or even just get the maximum benefit from an online presence.

–Shel Horowitz, book marketing/publishing consultant and award-winning author of *Grassroots Marketing for Authors and Publishers* (www.grassrootsmarketingforauthors.com)

An excellent book for authors looking to take control of their book marketing! From blogging to article marketing, from Facebook Page creation to thriving on Twitter, this book has it all!

–Vikram Narayan, CEO of BookBuzzr Book Marketing Technologies

Too few authors understand that social media isn't just about blasting out free commercials to sell books. It's about creating a larger-than-life profile online and making it easy for people who are hungry for your expertise and content to find you. Once they know, like and trust you, you've practically sold your book. Lorraine Phillips clearly "gets it." In *Online Book Marketing*, she gives authors an excellent overview of websites, including social media sites, where they must have a commanding presence. What separates this book from the dozens of other books that teach book marketing online? The accompanying 26-page workbook. It's the springboard you'll use to plan your entire marketing campaign.

–Joan Stewart, The Publicity Hound (PublicityHound.com)

Eyeballs have moved from print to online. This book leads you to where today's customers are. Save time, save money and make your marketing more effective.

–Dan Poynter, best-selling author of *The Self-Publishing Manual*

It isn't easy being an author. Not only do you have to write the book, but in today's marketplace, you have to market it as well. Your publisher can and will only do so much. The rest will depend on you. Which is why I highly recommend that you grab a copy of this book. Lorraine Phillips has done a great service to authors and would-be authors everywhere. She has created a guide that takes marketing a book from a vague concept to a scalable plan. Buy it. Highlight it. Implement it. You will be glad you did.

–Shama Kabani, best-selling author of *The Zen of Social Media Marketing*

Lorraine Phillips has written a book marketing manifesto. In order to sell any book these days, you must have a comprehensive online strategy, and this gives a step-by-step plan on exactly how to develop one. Smart authors will read this book before they even start writing!

–Melinda F. Emerson, small business expert and author of *Become Your Own Boss in 12 Months*

Online Book Marketing

The Least Expensive, Most Effective Ways to Create Book Buzz

By
Lorraine Phillips

360 Books

To download your
FREE Online Book Marketing Workbook
and to access direct links to ALL the resources
listed throughout this book, please visit

www.
online
book
buzz.
com

Find your username and password on page 195.

Interior layout and design by 360 Books (www.3sixtybooks.com)

Author: Lorraine Phillips
Editors: Jessica Radzak and Samantha Grace Dias

ISBN-10: 0982276559
ISBN-13: 9780982276556

LCCN: 2011920158
Library of Congress subject headings:
1. Internet marketing.
2. Reference books–Publishing.

Published by:
360 Books, LLC
C/O #22430
PO Box 105603
Atlanta, GA 30348-5603
www.3sixtybooks.com

First Printing
Printed in the United States of America

In loving memory of my Grandfather,
Lewis Ezekiel Phillips

May 4, 1917–February 11, 2011

Table of Contents

Part III. Social Media Marketing

Part IV. Other Vehicles for Online Marketing

Preface

There are two profound lessons that I have recently come to understand, and I would like to share them both with you. As an avid book reader, possibly even an addict, I have purchased numerous books covering many subjects in my time. I rarely read fiction, so when I'm interested in a particular subject, I hit the Internet to find out what's hot and what's not and purchase books, ebooks, products, courses, and CDs based on recommendations and testimonials. I also make evaluations based on excerpts that I am allowed to view or hear online.

Some of those products have been absolutely amazing, providing me with the information I need, helping me to grow, and enhancing my life in some way. Notice I said *some.* Others, even though they received the highest ratings from customers on Amazon and around the Internet, have been absolutely horrible. I couldn't believe how some products were rated so highly by so many given the information that was presented. I don't say this to be arrogant in any way. Maybe I took for granted some of the information I already knew, and that's why I could not find value in these products for me personally.

I also download conference calls, webinars, and podcasts that I can listen to while on the move. In one particular conference call, a gentleman (I will not give his name) called himself a coaching guru, but no matter how much I listened to him, I just felt that he was not providing answers to questions and that he kept reiterating the same spiel, in one form or another, of how his (very expensive) coaching course could help listeners achieve their goals. What surprised me, however, was how many people on that call got inspired (1) from just talking and connecting with him and (2) by the information he provided. You could hear the appreciation in their voices and the change in tone from when they got on the call to when it ended. They were fired up! I came to realize the following lesson as a result of this conference call.

LESSON 1: No matter what level or stage you are at in life, you can ALWAYS help somebody.

This was truly a humbling lesson for me personally. Being a true perfectionist, I had always felt that you had to know absolutely everything about something before you could take it to the masses. Maybe that's why so many of my past projects got stuck in planning for so long and not in doing. But this gentleman on the conference call helped me realize that no matter what, you can always make a difference in someone's life, even if it means you having to learn and grow along the way, too.

We've all heard of Web 2.0 and more recently Marketing 2.0, but I call it Love 2.0. Let me explain. The face of business is changing. Our economic world is changing. There are new rules that define both of these tenets; if these new rules are not followed, these institutions and systems will face extinction. Existing solely for profit and greed is no longer a sustainable and profitable business model. The world is changing, and this book has been created with that change in mind. Almost every chapter presented deals with you giving away–for FREE–valuable content in the form of information.

The Internet has reshaped our lives and everything around it. Yes, there are positives and negatives, but the big plus is that now you can share yourself and everything you know with more than just the immediate circle of people that surrounds you. From the comfort of your home and for the price of an Internet connection (which can sometimes even be FREE), your reach has now expanded across the globe–something that would have cost you thousands of dollars to do just a decade ago.

You have a passion that's genuine, you're knowledgeable about a particular subject, and it's something in your heart you know you were just born to do. Well, now you can talk about it till the cows come home. Even more gratifying, you can probably find an audience who actually wants to listen. What more reward do you want than that? You see...

LESSON 2: Your book is no longer a product. It simply exists as a BONUS to whatever else you have to offer.

And you've got to change the way you think about your book to that point of view as well. Love 2.0 is about sharing and being concerned with the general well-being of others. Don't you want to share your knowledge, expertise, and experience? Don't you want to enhance lives and make a difference? Don't you want to answer questions, solve problems, and provide solutions? This is about satisfying your customers' needs FIRST by giving helpful information away for FREE, and then, almost secondarily, you just happen to have a product for sale (because after all, you have to eat, too). That has to be the premise on which your business is built. And make no mistake, your book IS a business. I am reminded of a quote from Earl Nightingale that reads, "No man can get rich himself unless he enriches others."

Welcome to Love 2.0!

Introduction

As we all know, "push" or interruption marketing is dead. We've been bombarded with so many advertising messages over the years that we are now almost numb to them. Social media's growing dominance means that traditional marketers have to rethink their old strategies and instead turn to soft sell, content-driven marketing strategies. They are now less promotional and more personal, engaging customers on their own terms; speaking their language; and providing helpful, relevant information that not only demonstrates expertise, but puts their customers' needs first. As authors, we need to interact with our readers in the same way–fulfilling their content needs with more than just the books we have on offer.

It's a well-known fact that most people turn to search engines to look for information, products, professionals, and services more than any other medium out there. The best form of consistent, high-quality traffic to a website will come from a search engine, and Google accounts for over 60 percent of the total search market. Knowing this, it makes perfect sense to solely focus your efforts on improving your rankings in Google, because if your information doesn't show up there, then you can't be found, and you won't get the business. Plus, I think it's safe to assume that most other engines closely mimic Google's indexing and ranking technologies anyway.

If Google is the number one engine used to search for information online, Amazon is the number one website used to purchase books or other products online, making it a number one authority site that shows consistently and ranks high for numerous categories in Google results. Simply having a book that is listed and categorized with appropriate keywords on Amazon is by far the most effective "ad" (that isn't even really perceived as an ad) that you can have for your book. Although outside the scope of this book (there are many great offerings that will tell you how to get listed on Amazon), if you are going to take your online marketing activities to the max, then getting your book accurately listed on Amazon is one activity that you need to ensure is performed.

If your readers are online and looking for solutions to problems that your book solves, then it is absolutely imperative that they can easily find you. It's up to you to take advantage of every possible means you have to reach them, whether through search engines, Amazon, social media, websites, blogs, articles, newsletters, podcasts, videos, press releases, or other means. There are many options available, and as vast and ever-changing as the Internet is, it was absolutely impossible for me to cover every single one or describe every single feature offered. What you have in this book is definitely not an exhaustive guide, but I have selected the avenues that I feel are the most advantageous for authors to connect with their readers and build relationships online.

Although the information presented is current today (as of this writing), due to the nature of the Internet, it may not be that way tomorrow. For this reason, a lot of my attention has been given to underlying principles, ideas, and strategies that should remain the same no matter how the technologies built on top change. Don't even attempt to try to do all the strategies presented. Although you should never rely solely on one method, pick the ones that are appropriate for your audience and the ones you find most enjoyable to use because if you're not enjoying it, then I would say that it's just not worth the effort.

As you read through the chapters of this book, think of ways you can repurpose your content so that it appears across different platforms as well as in numerous formats. Can you turn your book into a series of articles? Can you turn a collection of blog posts into a book? How about turning a text article into an audio podcast? Or a PowerPoint presentation into a video that includes audio commentary? Creatively reuse your content in a way that allows you to reach a much larger audience as you cater to people's different learning styles.

This book is not made to be read in any particular order. However, I do suggest that you read it in its entirety, as the ideas presented are not mutually exclusive to each chapter. You may read an idea in the author blog chapter that you decide to use for your podcast, or you may read an idea from the Twitter chapter that you decide to use for email marketing purposes. I highly recommend that you start by reading the first three chapters, as they present the basic principles on which ALL other methods and activities will be based. Chapter 3 will be the most technical, as we will delve into a little HTML so that you might understand search engine optimization (SEO) techniques that can be used in ALL your online marketing activities. I've given you just enough information to be dangerous, and that you will be by the end of this book.

In closing, I hope that you find this reference and guide to be most useful. I had an absolute blast writing it.

Wishing you every success,

Lorraine Phillips, Author

PART I

Your Brand, Your Book, and You

Chapter 1:

What Is a Brand?

Everything is judged by its appearance; what is unseen counts for nothing. Never let yourself get lost in the crowd, then, or buried in oblivion. Stand out. Be conspicuous, at all cost. Make yourself a magnet of attention by appearing larger, more colorful, more mysterious, than the bland and timid masses.
—Robert Greene, *The 48 Laws of Power*

A brand is the specific identity of a product, service, or business. It is the emotional and psychological relationship that you have with your customers and the promise you make that is distinguished by a distinctive characteristic such as a name, logo, sign, trademark, symbol, color combination, jingle, or slogan.

A strong brand that is communicated well means that when a customer thinks of a particular product or service, they think of you or your business first. It's what you use to stand out and set yourself apart from the competition. Wal-Mart's "Everyday Low Prices," Nike's "Just Do It," and Burger King's "Your Way Right Away" are all excellent examples of great slogans (along with powerful symbols) that have been used to create rock-solid brand identities in the marketplace.

So now you're thinking, "Okay, I get this branding thing, but I'm an author. What's that got to do with me?" Well, I am here to tell you that if you want to sell books, and I mean *really* sell books, then branding has everything to do with you. Let's say you've written a book about improving your golf swing. Although you know that yours is the best in the market, there are about ten thousand other books (not to mention ebooks) that talk about the same thing. So how do you distinguish yourself from the competition? The answer is by your brand. It's the one thing you have that can never be duplicated because, quite simply, your brand is YOU.

In today's world, with the advent of Internet marketing, brands have become extremely personal, which means that a brand now has a personality, and that personality includes a voice. Lucky for you, your voice is unique. Literally, there is no one out there quite like you–from the tone of your voice to the things that you say, the way that you think, your particular point of view, how you feel, the ideas you have, and the way that you express yourself. Your personal brand represents the real you, and it is ultimately what people want to connect with. They want to learn from, or do business with, someone they can relate to and identify with; someone who understands their wants, needs, frustrations, dreams, fears, and aspirations; and most importantly, someone who can provide uncomplicated solutions to their perceived problems or information needs. Could that someone possibly be you?

Your brand has to be totally believable, engaging, and relevant, delivering content that is vital to your target audience's needs. The more you personalize and relate, the more approachable you will be. Every interaction, regardless of the medium used, will give you the opportunity to develop a relationship in a way that can turn casual readers into loyal ones.

Now that I have your interest and attention, I know you are wondering, "Well, how do I go about creating a brand?" And my answer to you would be, "Well, who are you?" Because once you define that, then you can take it to the bank. To help you think about and create your personal brand, I have devised a set of questions you need to answer. These questions will assist you in thinking not only about who you are, but also about who your potential readers are and why they should take an interest in your book. After all, you will be creating your brand with your readers' needs and interests in mind.

It's imperative to understand your readers so that you might make a personal connection and satisfy their informational needs. Whether writing your newsletter, creating your website, posting on Facebook, or tweeting on Twitter, you want to ensure that you are effectively communicating a brand that stamps your promise to readers every time. To get the branding process under way, grab a pen and write down the answers to the following questions. You will also find these questions listed in the FREE workbook available at www.onlinebookbuzz.com.

About You

1. Who are you, and what do you do?
2. What qualifies you to be an authority on your subject (i.e., experience, qualifications, training, etc.)?
3. What natural talents and abilities do you bring to your work?
4. What is different, unique, or special about you?
5. What do people always tell you you're good at?
6. What qualities do you admire most about yourself?
7. What are your five highest values in life? What's most important to you? What do you stand for?
8. What are you most passionate about as it relates to your work?
9. What do you want to achieve through your work?
10. What is your ultimate purpose?
11. Who would you like the public to perceive you as, or what would you like to be known for?

About Your Readers

1. Who are your readers?
2. Where are they located? How will you find or reach them both online and offline?

3. What kind of organizations do they belong to?
4. What types of events do they attend?
5. What publications do they read?
6. What is it that they want to know? What are some of their interests, problems, frustrations, concerns, dreams, aspirations, and fears?

About Your Book

1. What is your book's genre or category?
2. How does your book benefit its readers? What problems does it solve? What needs or desires does it fulfill?
3. Where else can your reader find the answers that your book contains (e.g., other books, magazines, websites, blogs, DVDs, audio programs, etc.)?
4. In relation to these other mediums, how is your book different, and what does it do better? Why should somebody buy your book?

Chapter 2: Optimizing Your Book for Online Sales

Your Book's Title and Subtitle

Your book is the cornerstone of your brand, and your book's title is the promise you make to your readers. It's the first thing they'll see, whether on the front of the cover, in an Internet search engine, or on your author site. Therefore, your title is the most important online marketing tool you possess. Your title should be no longer than five or six words. Keeping the number of words to a minimum allows for the title to be displayed in a large, attention-grabbing font on the front cover.

An effective title needs to arrestingly communicate the correct message to your desired audience, and it should be all of the following:

- Accurate
- Descriptive
- Relevant
- Persuasive
- Easy to understand

- Memorable
- Catchy
- Compelling
- Clear
- Direct
- Specific
- Concise

Your book title should immediately answer the reader's question of "What's in it for me?" (WIIFM), appealing to their self-interest by either providing a solution to a problem or by offering compelling information or relevant news. It is absolutely imperative that you understand who your readers are and what their needs are so that you can craft a message that speaks directly to them. Although your book may contain the best information, if your title does not capture a reader's attention, he or she may never get to read what's on the inside.

When deciding on your book's title, hop over to Go Daddy (www.godaddy.com) and check to see if that domain name is available. Get creative and check variations of the title if you need to. I am a dot-com fanatic and refuse to use .net, .org, .info, .biz, or any other variation currently being offered, but that's just my personal preference. After deciding on the title for this book, I discovered the URL was not available. Plus, I felt that it was too long, so I opted for www.onlinebookbuzz.com. It was close enough to the title, conveyed what the book is about, could easily be remembered, and contained a couple of my keywords.

Note: For more information on choosing a domain, please see my top ten rules for selecting a domain name on page 42.

Your subtitle is another critical piece of online marketing real estate that should never be just an afterthought. It's the second sound bite of your book. Its purpose is to expound on, or further explain, your title, giving more information about the book and convincing readers that it's the one for them. Because of the way book information is cataloged and stored in various databases online, try to keep your subtitle no longer than 110 characters.

When creating your title and subtitle, you should make sure that either one or both contain "keyword" phrases that will help improve the visibility of your book in search engine results. Keywords are words or phrases that determine which category a site will be listed under in search engine results or the terms that an Internet user might use to search for information on a particular topic or subject. For instance, if looking for information on "online book marketing," a user might perform a search on any of the following terms and permutations:

Online book marketing
Book marketing online
Marketing online
Online marketing
Marketing books online
Marketing books on the Internet
Online book promotion
Promoting a book online
Book promotion
Internet book marketing
Book marketing
Internet book publicity
Web marketing for books

Your job is to find out the most common phrase used to search for your particular subject and include it within the title or subtitle, aiming not to repeat words in the subtitle that you have already used in your title. Lucky for us, search engine companies like Google and Yahoo! log the statistics of all searches performed online, and there are keyword research tools (as will be discussed in Chapter 3's "Keyword Research Strategies" on page 49) that you can use to look up the most common phrases or terms used to search for your particular subject on the Net.

The Cover

Next on our hit list is the cover. After discovering your book online and clicking on the link provided, this is more than likely the second impression of your book that your potential readers will see. Your cover must work in unison with your title (and subtitle), so it must effectively, accurately, and immediately convey your book's message.

Although it is said that you can't judge a book by its cover, potential readers will. In their minds, if your cover looks good, then there's a good chance that the contents will be also. It is said that consumers "buy with their eyes," and magazine consumer studies estimate that the cover and cover design is the number one factor driving newsstand sales, accounting for at least 75 percent of all single-copy sales. I think it's safe to assume that book purchasers also take your cover design just as seriously.

With that in mind, it is important for you to have the cover professionally designed. You've taken weeks, months, maybe even years to complete your manuscript, so don't let your book down with an unprofessional, amateurish-looking cover. This is not the place for you to cut costs or corners. Your cover is an important marketing tool and one of your ultimate selling points. Readers, retailers, and reviewers alike will give your cover just a few seconds before making a judgment or purchase decision, so it should immediately grab attention, or at the very least, rouse interest. An experienced designer can create an eye-catching design that ensures the following:

- Your cover stands out in the crowd.
- It effectively conveys the book's message.
- It is visually attractive.
- It looks professional.
- It's memorable.
- It appeals to your target audience.
- It has a poster-like appearance.
- It's an original design.

- The graphic, title, and subtitle display clearly and legibly no matter what size the cover is displayed at online.

Remember, the objective of a visually appealing front cover is to entice the reader to

- read the back cover,
- look at the table of contents,
- skim or browse the actual contents,
- give it a review, or
- make a purchase.

These are objectives that I do not feel should be left to chance. If you don't know of any great designers yourself (and I said great, not good), then check the various freelance resources available online. Here's a list to start you off.

Elance (www.elance.com)
Freelancer (www.freelancer.com)
Guru (www.guru.com)

Personally, I have had much success using Elance. It's quick and easy to get signed up and post your project online. After you've done that, all you have to do is sit back and let the designers find you. When deciding on a designer, scrutinize their portfolio to ensure that their work exemplifies the style, flair, and design characteristics you are looking for. Know that there are many differences in the technical aspects of creating a book cover for a book that will appear in print as well as in ebook or digital format. I suggest you don't concern yourself with terms like CMYK, RGB, bleed, vector images, raster images, and dots per inch (dpi). Instead, put your energy and focus into the actual marketing of your book.

Your Back Cover Copy

After your potential readers have checked out your title and looked at your cover, they will hopefully be enticed to read the synopsis on the back, which will be summarized online. Once again, you are presented with another opportunity to sell, sell, sell your book. What will readers get out of reading your book? What benefit, advantage, or reward will they receive? What problems do you solve? What types of solutions do you provide? What knowledge will they gain that they don't already have?

Answering these questions will allow readers to evaluate whether to buy your book and whether it will be worth the investment of both their money and time. Here are some examples of the things that people want:

- To be entertained
- To lead more self-fulfilling lives
- To find love and commitment
- To build a strong self-image
- To achieve better health and longer lives
- To be more attractive to the opposite sex
- To attain financial security and wealth
- To receive buying advice on products and services
- To know how to save time and be more efficient
- To be self-sufficient, including owning their own business
- To understand their place in the overall scheme of things
- To gain clarity and direction
- To be motivated and inspired
- To find inner peace
- To be successful
- To gain knowledge or expertise in a certain field

Ultimately, your readers are looking for ways to enhance their lives in some way, shape, or form. Make sure you address these types of needs by highlighting one to five benefits that your book provides. Have a descriptive summary that includes a bullet point list of benefits as well as reviews and testimonials. Your word count should be between 100 and 150 words long, not including the brief author summary you may also provide. Make every word and phrase count! Oh, and last but not least, make it "keyword rich," as you will most likely also be using this copy on your author site as well as numerous other places online.

PART II

Your Author Site and Blog

Chapter 3:
Your Author Site

Your author site should be the foundation of any great online marketing plan. Working for you twenty-four hours a day, seven days a week, all around the world, your author site allows you to further establish your name and extend your brand. The content AND appearance of your website are the most important factors when determining its value. To succeed online, it must be both eye-catching and professional.

It is important that your message be specific and that you let your audience know exactly what you're offering, always answering their question of "What's in it for me?" Create your site based on THEIR needs (not yours). If you want visitors to come back, then you will have to give them a reason for doing so by featuring compelling, relevant, useful content that is updated regularly. They say, "Content is king," but I say, "*Great* content is king." And the more content or pages you have, the more times you will appear under the search results for a certain topic.

Make your site as interactive as possible by giving readers things to do. Include polls, questionnaires, surveys, and occasional contests. Your content should encourage conversation and get users to interact by submitting their comments and opinions. Know that your readers are looking for a connection, not only with you, but with other readers who share their same interests, so your site should accommodate for that, too.

Having an author site allows you to:

- Increase awareness about your book (or upcoming books)
- Increase book sales
- Share excerpts or sample chapters
- Establish brand credibility
- Display testimonials, reviews, and endorsements
- Showcase your credentials and bio information
- Further position yourself as an expert (remembering to answer the question from Chapter 1, "Who would you like the public to perceive you as, or what would you like to be known for?")
- Feature rich multimedia content, such as graphics, photos, video, animation, and audio
- Find your target audience and help your target audience find you
- Build and maintain a loyal following
- Build your email marketing list
- Collect demographic and psychographic information about your audience
- Communicate directly through email messages and newsletters
- Publicize your Facebook, Twitter, LinkedIn, and YouTube accounts, giving readers other ways to connect with you online
- Link to or incorporate your blog or vlog (video log)
- Share any upcoming events or personal appearances
- Create a press room where the media and other users can download or view your media kit and press releases
- Market and sell any ancillary products you may have created as spin-offs from your book, such as ebooks, CDs, DVDs, instructional guides, workbooks, or podcasts
- Advertise any professional services you may offer, such as public speaking, consultation, teaching, and coaching
- Provide contact information (email, phone, Skype, etc.) so that readers, reviewers, interviewers, and press are able to reach you directly

I hope you see the value of creating an author site for your book and how it can further enhance your online marketing efforts. It's really the place that you call home. Your online brochure, if you please, where you get to tell readers who you are and why they need you (or your book) in their lives.

Choosing Your Host and Registering Your Domain

Your host's function is to store your site, or the physical HTML web pages you create, on its servers and display those pages over the Web. Your registrar is the company through which you will register your domain name, or the name of your author site. Your host and registrar can be the same provider, or they can be separate. If you decide to purchase a hosting plan from a provider that is different from your registrar, then your host will give you the directions you need to point your domain to its servers so that you can physically host and administer your site with them. Either way, it's a simple, quick, and easy process.

Over the past fifteen years, I have built websites for clients using many different hosts, and the one I can highly recommend is Just Host (www.justhost.com). Their hosting plans start at $4.45 per month, and I can tell you, the features offered just can't be beat. You get a free domain for life (so no extra domain registration fees); unlimited website space (which means that if you need to upload a trillion videos, you can); unlimited streaming or data transfer; unlimited email accounts; free WordPress, Joomla, and osCommerce installation; and worldwide 24/7 technical support that includes live chat. If that wasn't enough, there is also an anytime money-back guarantee. Just Host provides a simple, intuitive user interface (or control panel) that you use to administer your site. In addition, you receive unlimited domain hosting, which means you can host multiple domains on a single account, so you'll never need to purchase another hosting plan no matter how many websites you decide to create in the future.

Regarding your domain, make sure that you actually own it and that you are not just tagging onto somebody else's name or brand. If purchasing a plan from Just Host (or any other hosting provider that offers this feature), then you will have the option of registering your domain name for FREE. I prefer going this route, as it means that my registrar and host are one and the same, which just makes things a little easier down the line. If you are not ready to purchase a hosting plan but would still like to secure your domain name, then I suggest registering at Go Daddy (www.godaddy.com).

Note: Tweexchange (www.tweexchange.com) allows you to search both Twitter names and domain names (through Go Daddy) simultaneously. As you type in a name, the box underneath displays a side-by-side comparison of what's available and what's not for each. A Twitter username can only be up to fifteen characters in length, so if you're going for a longer domain, then it will be necessary for you to create a variation of that name to use on Twitter.

Here are my top ten rules for selecting a domain name:

1. It should be a dot-com.
2. It should be as close as possible to either your full name or your book's title (taking into consideration your title's length).
3. If not using your name or book title, then your URL should be somewhat descriptive so that people don't have to totally guess what your book is about.
4. It should include your keywords or keyword phrases.
5. It should be reflective of your brand.
6. It should be reasonably short.
7. It should be catchy, easy to remember, and easy to say.
8. It should not contain any underscores, as links are often highlighted or underlined, making a URL that contains an underscore somewhat hard to read.
9. Unless you absolutely have to, it should not contain more than one hyphen. If using your name as your domain, then I suggest

you purchase both the non-hyphenated and hyphenated versions. As in the case of a site called Who Represents (www.whorepresents.com), they might have been better off purchasing the hyphenated version, so the address would have read www.who-represents.com.

10. It should not be confusing and difficult to find (i.e., not the .net or .org name of an already existing and established .com site).

They say that rules are meant to be broken, but try to stick to these guidelines as much as possible. As always, use your best judgment and go with what feels right to you.

Creating Your Site

In this day and age, there are many methods that can be used to create a website. For the purposes of our discussion, I will focus on a few of the options that are available to you.

Build it yourself from scratch

Unless you are truly familiar with web design principles, a master at computer languages (e.g., HTML, CSS, Perl, Ajax, and PHP), as well as a skilled graphic designer, I do not recommend that you go this route. Web design covers many disciplines–which evolve daily–and it will take considerable time to not only learn each one, but also to learn how to integrate them successfully. Forget picking up any of those *HTML for Dummies* type books. You should be (or at least you will be by the end of this book) busy enough with your online marketing activities. For this option, I strongly advise that you just say no!

Use a web template

There are various online services that offer HTML, CSS, and Flash templates for download. Although they look impressive and easy to use, as an experienced designer, I can tell you that they are not. You will have to customize these templates to fit your particular needs, and because of the design constraints, it is often like trying to fit a square peg into a round hole. Take a good look; pictures are a certain size, and text fits into designated areas. Unless you are experienced with preparing materials for the web, your template will turn out looking completely different from what you had expected. While working for a design firm in Atlanta, I knew of several clients who thought they had done the simplest, quickest, cheapest thing and had bypassed designer fees by purchasing a template, but they ended up back at square one and had to hire the company to customize their rather complicated template. If you decide to use a template, then factor in that you may also need to hire a designer to help with customization.

Hire a web designer

This is the most expensive option, but if you don't value your brand, then no one else will. Professional web designers specialize in presenting information (or content) in a way that is functional, efficient, and aesthetically pleasing. Your site must be built around audience needs, so make sure it is easy for them to navigate and find relevant information quickly. We've all visited those hideous, frustrating websites, never to return again–which is exactly what we don't want to happen here. Hire a designer who has the skills, knowledge, and experience to implement the design and features you desire. If you don't know of any professional designers, check the freelance resources, such as Elance (www.elance.com), that are available online. See Appendix A on page 181 for a list of questions to ask your web designer or web design firm.

Create an author profile

As a complete alternative–or, I suggest, in addition–to your author website, there are sites that allow you to create an author platform where you can build a profile that consists of your bio, blog, trailer, podcast, videos, and images. These sites also let you showcase and present your book information for promotional purposes. These communities allow writers, authors, publishers, readers, reviewers, and book buyers to connect–discovering, discussing, and reviewing books; building reading lists; and providing book recommendations. You can never be in too many places on the web, so I suggest joining and creating profiles at all of the following sites (and just so you know, FiledBy is my favorite).

AuthorsDen (www.authorsden.com)
bookhitch.com (www.bookhitch.com)
FiledBy (www.filedby.com)
Goodreads (www.goodreads.com)
LibraryThing (www.librarything.com)
Nothing Binding (www.nothingbinding.com)
PolkaDotBanner (www.polkadotbanner.com)
Published.com (www.published.com)
Red Room (www.redroom.com)
Shelfari (www.shelfari.com)

Why You Should Hire a Web Designer

Hiring a professional designer can help you avoid the following web faux pas:

- Non-branded, inconsistent, and incohesive design
- A website that is not targeted toward a particular audience (e.g., a site aimed at teens should look and feel different from a site aimed at retirees)
- Cluttered design
- Unclear navigation where users cannot easily recognize what page they are on or identify where they need to go

- Nondescriptive navigation that does not clearly communicate the information contained on each page
- Frustrating menus that do not work or that function incorrectly
- Important pages or relevant information (such as book purchase information or the "Contact" page) that are hard to find or buried too deep within the site
- Lack of contrast or use of an unpleasing color scheme
- Colored, complex, distracting backgrounds
- Overuse of annoying, blinking, flashing banner ads or graphics
- Difficult-to-read text because of the background color, text size, or text color
- The use of fonts not available on all computers, resulting in the site looking different depending on which platform or device is being used to view the site
- Slow-loading pages and graphics
- Background music that does not include a start or stop button
- Orphan pages that do not provide a way back to the originating page, forcing users to click the browser's "Back" button
- Broken links that either do nothing or that lead nowhere, resulting in the "Page Cannot Be Found" error
- "Under Construction" or "Coming Soon" pages
- Vertical scrolling
- Browser incompatibility, where your site displays and acts differently depending on which browser, browser version, platform, or device is being used to view it
- Not using effective SEO techniques, making it very difficult for users to learn about you and discover your site

INFORMATION YOUR WEB DESIGNER NEEDS

When deciding on your site design, it will be necessary for you to be as specific as possible. Let your designer know exactly what you would like, including the features you need and the particular style you have in mind. Let your designer know what your book is about and the particular audience it is aimed at. Reference the information you compiled in Chapter 1 regarding your audience, your book, and your brand. Really think through these types of questions, so your designer can provide a solution that works best for you.

The look of your site. How should your website look? Professional, trendy, technical, stylish, friendly, modern, hip, businesslike, feminine, fun, bold, cutting edge, trustworthy, informative? Putting together about eight adjectives that describe the theme best suited to your particular audience will aid tremendously in your site's design and implementation. What colors do you like? What colors do you dislike? Do you have any sites that your designer can use for reference? Provide URLs of both sites you like and sites you dislike.

The functionality of your site. What functionality will you require? A newsletter sign-up form, blog, chat room, polls, surveys, downloadable items, contact forms, an online store where your book can be purchased, or links to Amazon and other book outlets? Will your site be static or dynamic?

The content of your site. What should your site communicate? What are you trying to achieve? Who will be responsible for updating the content? How often will it be updated?

Lastly, decide on the number of pages you would like and give the names of the pages that will appear as the navigational links. Ideas for pages include "About the Book," "Table of Contents," "Testimonials," "Downloads," "About the Author," "Services," "My Blog," "Press Room," and "Contact."

Pay particular attention to the content that appears on your home page. This is the most important and most powerful page on your site, as more often than not, the information presented there (and the design) will determine whether a user continues to peruse through the rest of the site. If landing at your site through a web search, then your visitor was more likely looking for general information about a subject than buying a physical book about it. Use your copy to market your message and not your book. Answer the searcher's query by boldly proclaiming the benefits and solutions your book provides right there on your home page. Aim to convert that searcher into a buyer. Don't let potential customers get away! If all else fails, then at least they will be tempted to sign up for your irresistible newsletter offer that contains some of the information they need. Work it!

Creating Search Engine Friendly Web Pages

Search engine optimization (SEO) is the official term for improving the visibility of a website or web page in search engine results. Search engines work by sending out automated programs, called spiders or robots, that crawl the Internet, visiting sites, reading the information found there, and then indexing this information by storing the results in a database. Crawlers refresh these indexes at different intervals, periodically returning to sites to check for updated content. Storing the data this way allows for quick searches online; otherwise bots would have to physically crawl the Internet every time a search is performed. I couldn't even begin to imagine how long a method like that would take to complete today.

Making your website search engine friendly simply means that a web page has been coded in a way that makes it easily accessible to these crawlers, explicitly and clearly providing the specific information they look for as well as presenting that information in the best possible manner. There are two primary methods used by search engines for finding, indexing, and cataloging your site:

1. Keywords, which allow each page on your website to be relevant for particular search terms
2. Meta tags, which are special HTML or XML tags that provide information about the contents of a web page, as explained in "Placing Keywords Within HTML Meta Tags" on page 51

KEYWORD RESEARCH STRATEGIES

Your job is to find out the most common phrase(s) used to search for your particular subject matter and include those terms as keywords on your web page so that you might rank higher in search results, thereby increasing your chances of actually being found on the Web. When creating your list of keywords, try not to be too general. Remember, you are competing with a trillion other websites out there, so it's important to be as specific as possible.

Never use one-word keywords, as this will guarantee you don't get high rankings. For instance, if your website focuses on golf swings, don't just use the word "golf" as a keyword. Instead, use phrases such as "golf swing tips," "golf swing instructions," "golf swing training," or "improving your golf swing."

When researching the best keywords to use for your particular niche, take "long tail keywords" into consideration. Long tail keywords consist of three or more words that are the less common, less competitive keywords searched for but that can be responsible for delivering significant levels of high-quality, targeted traffic to your site. For instance, the specific phrase "Canon PowerShot Digital Camera," as opposed to the more general "digital camera," indicates that the searcher knows exactly what he or she is looking for and is probably ready to take some type of action, whether that means making a purchase, downloading a report, or signing up for a newsletter. Focusing on less popular terms can also increase your site's chances of being highly ranked for your selected keyword phrase.

To clearly define what your audience searches for, spend some time browsing the web visiting similar sites, competitor sites, forums, chat rooms, newsgroups, or blogs where your potential customers hang out. (That's why it is important to know your target audience.) Take note of the types of problems discussed and the kinds of words and phrases used, making sure to jot down any recurring themes you find. Plug these phrases into a keyword research tool to see what other keywords or phrases you come up with. Cross-check your results by repeating the exercise in at least one other tool to see if you can generate more options. If using Google AdWords, you can also plug your URL or a competitor's URL into the website field for a list of suggested keywords. Compile a list of keywords you find that are not too competitive and that appear most consistently across results.

Keyword Research Tools

FREE Services
Google AdWords (https://adwords.google.com)
Google Insights (www.google.com/insights/search/#cmpt=q)
SEMRush (de.semrush.com)
Wordtracker (https://freekeywords.wordtracker.com)

Paid Services with Free Trials
Keyword Discovery (www.keyworddiscovery.com)
Wordtracker (www.wordtracker.com)

Another suggestion I have is to head over to Amazon and do a search for books that appear in the same category or genre as yours. Selecting the first two or three books on the list, scroll down to the section on the page that reads, "Tags Customers Associate with This Product." Jot these terms down also. Amazon is the most frequently visited site for shopping for a product online, so it will help you to know the tags (or phrases) that customers themselves associate with your particular book category.

Most importantly, you should be learning from the competition. To do this, enter any of the keyword phrases from the list you have now compiled into your favorite search engine and note the sites that show up in the top set of results that closely match your content offerings. Head over to ABAKUS Topword (www.abakus-Internet-marketing.de/tools/topword.htm) and enter each of the URLs you have found.

This amazing tool analyzes the top keywords in a web page, providing you with a list of the most used single keywords, two-word phrases, and three-word phrases that can be found on a page. Once again, look for similarities and differences between these results and what you have already found. Using the information you have compiled from these strategies, create a final master keyword list that consists of at least six to ten phrases you can use as target phrases on the various pages throughout your site.

It is important to know that search engines read your web page from the top down. Aim to place your keyword phrases at the very top of the page (if you can, before the main header or navigation), toward the front of your first set of paragraphs, and continue to sprinkle them throughout the content of your page. All pages on your site should be optimized for a specific search term, with your home page being optimized for your most important keyword phrase. This strategy allows the pages in your site to rank for several keyword terms (instead of just one), and it also eliminates the possibility of the pages within your site competing against one another for particular terms.

Always ensure that your content is relevant, unique, interesting, and useful to visitors. Don't try to stuff so many keywords in that your content becomes nonsensical. Although you're aiming to make your pages search engine friendly, your first order of business is to ensure your page is readable in a way that makes complete sense to your audience. If they are unable to make heads or tails out of what you're saying, then they won't be visitors for long. Attempting to overstuff content with keyword phrases (and other questionable SEO tactics, such as attempting to hide keywords by making your text color the same as the color of your background) is known as "black hat search engine optimization," and is generally frowned upon by most search engines.

PLACING KEYWORDS WITHIN HTML META TAGS

Now we're about to get technical! Although these actions may be performed by your web designer, it is important that *you* understand this information for the following reasons:

1. To ensure that either you or your designer knows about and is actually building web pages that are coded correctly and are search engine friendly
2. To ensure that you can have an intelligible conversation (with your designer or another party) regarding the subject matter
3. To ensure that you create effective, appropriate "titles" and "meta tags" for each web page on your site (as will be discussed)
4. To ensure that you apply these principles to ALL the online marketing activities you may perform, whether it be social media marketing; blogging; creating articles, newsletters, podcasts, or video; or releasing a press release

Grab a pen or pencil and go line by line through the HTML code presented in Figure 2 until you truly understand what is going on. Depending on your level (we all have to start somewhere), it may be necessary for you to read this section over a few times. Have patience. I promise that if you take it slowly, you will eventually get it. So here goes...

HTML is a computer language that is used to define the structure and layout of a web page on the Internet. This language tells your browser how to display words and images on a web page by using code that contains a variety of "tags" and "attributes."

Tags are HTML commands that provide instructions to a browser. They usually come in pairs like <p> and </p>, where the first tag is called an opening tag and the second (that always includes a backslash) a closing tag. Just so you know, the <p> tag tells a browser to start or open a new paragraph, and the </p> tag tells the browser to close it.

An attribute allows you to further specify the particular characteristic of a certain tag. For a real-world example, if a tag were a dress suit, then the attributes could be blue color, wool fabric, medium size, and gold buttons. This is about as technical as you will need to get, and the clarification of these terms will become more apparent as we progress through this section.

Imagine you saw the following information displayed on a web page in a browser window:

Figure 1: Browser Window Display

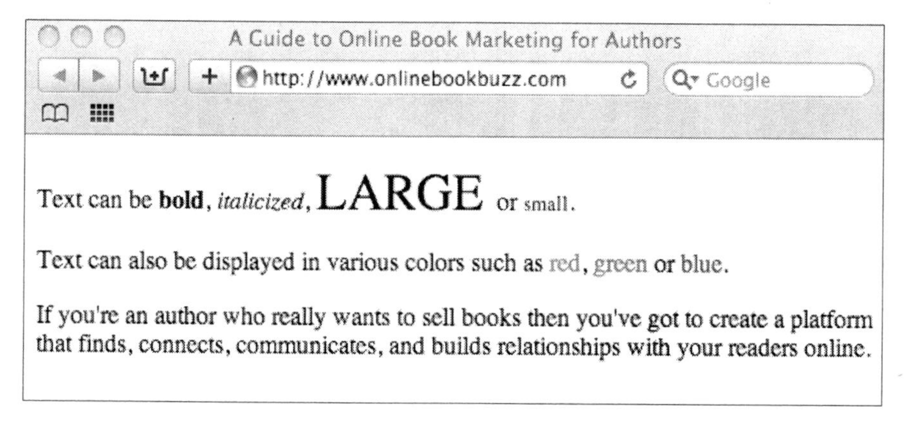

Visualize the word *red* being red, *green* being green, and *blue* being blue. See the HTML presented overleaf to view the code that has been used to construct the web page above.

The "**DOCTYPE**" declaration is always the first instruction that appears in an HTML document. It tells your browser what particular version of the markup language the page is written in.

The "**html xmlns**" statement tells the browser what language standards have been implemented on the page, and in our case, these standards can be found at http://www.w3.org/1999/xhtml.

The information contained within the "**head**" tags (<head> opens the tag, and </head> closes it) provides important information that is used by search engines to catalog and index your site. Note that the information contained within this tag is not actually displayed on the page by the browser.

Skipping to the "title" tag, it reads, "A Guide to Online Book Marketing for Authors." This tag is extremely important because search engines use this tag as one of the primary means for cataloging your site. When someone does an online search and your site is returned in the results, this will be the text of the clickable link that is presented. Make it descriptive, informative, and inviting so that your link is the one clicked on as opposed to the others that also appear in the search results. As you can see, this title is also displayed at the top of the browser window when a user actually visits the page, and this is the text that will be used when someone bookmarks the page or adds it as a favorite. Note that the title tag should be unique for every page on your site and fewer than 70 characters in length.

The next set of tags within the head are called "**meta tags**," and they are also very important. The "**description**" attribute includes a brief one- or two-sentence description of the page, and is the text that will be displayed underneath the clickable link in search results. The information you provide here allows people to determine whether your page contains the information they need. To avoid signs of keyword stuffing on the page, DO NOT use the same keywords found in your title tag. Aim to vary the description presented for each page by providing a brief summary of the content that appears on that particular page. To avoid being truncated in returned search results, make the description approximately 150 characters in length, including spaces.

Finally, we hit gold! The "**keywords**" attribute lists the words or phrases that best describe a particular page, enabling search engines to accurately categorize your site. Use synonyms, plurals, different permutations, and commonly misspelled words (e.g., *optimization* and *optimisation*, or *jewellery*, *jewelery*, and *jewelry*). Keyword prominence plays a critical role in determining your site's ranking, so PUT YOUR MOST IMPORTANT KEYWORDS UP FRONT. A keyword that appears at the beginning of the meta tag will have a prominence rating of 100 percent, keywords towards the middle around 50 percent, and keywords at the end about 0 percent. Your list should be no more than 250 characters, including commas and spaces.

Continuing with our example, the "**body**" tag defines all the contents that will actually be displayed by the browser, such as text, hyperlinks, images, videos, tables, and lists; describing not only the what, but also the how. Pages should be information AND keyword rich, specially designed to contain the most popular, most likely keywords that people will use to search for your site online.

When using keywords, you should also consider keyword proximity. Keyword proximity refers to the closeness between two or more keywords,

Figure 2: HTML Code

```
<!DOCTYPE html PUBLIC "-//W3C//DTD XHTML 1.0
     Transitional//EN" "http://www.w3.org/TR/
     xhtml1/DTD/xhtml1-transitional.dtd">
<html xmlns="http://www.w3.org/1999/xhtml">

<head>
  <meta http-equiv="Content-Type" content="text/
       html; charset=UTF-8" />
  <title>A Guide to Online Book Marketing for
       Authors</title>
  <meta name="description" content="Find the least
       expensive, most effective ways to create
       book buzz">
  <meta name="keywords" content="online book
       marketing, book marketing online, marketing
       a book, book marketing strategy, book
       marketing strategies, marketing books
       online, online book promotion, internet book
       marketing, book internet marketing, book
       marketing tips, book marketing ideas, book
       internet strategies">
</head>

<body>
  <p>Text can be <strong>bold</strong>,
       <em>italicized</em>, <font size=+3>LARGE
       </font> or <font size=-1>small</font>.</p>
  <p>Text can also be displayed in various
       colors such as <font color="red">red,
       </font> <font color="green">green</font>
        or <font color="blue">blue</font>.</p>
  <p>If you're an author who really wants to
       sell books then you've got to create a
       platform that finds, connects, communicates,
       and builds relationships with your readers
       online.</p>
</body>

</html>
```

with the general consensus being the closer the keywords, the better the results. For instance, "IT support services for small business" would be more effective than "We provide IT support services and only work strictly with small businesses." When at all possible, avoid using filler words between phrases.

> **Note:** Aim to use keyword phrases in your web page's headline and subhead tags, namely, the H1, H2, and H3 tags. Use your main keyword, with or without extra words, in the H1 tag and then use H2 and H3 to further breakdown the elements of your topic-centered page.

As a general rule of thumb, YOUR KEYWORD PHRASES SHOULD BE NO MORE THAN 7 PERCENT OF THE TOTAL NUMBER OF WORDS PRESENTED ON A PAGE. If there are more than that, then you risk appearing as a keyword spammer to search engines, which can result in your page being penalized or even totally excluded from search results. To help you measure the number of times your keyword phrases appear on a page, see the "Keyword Density Analyzer Tools" section on page 59.

Understand that there is no magic bullet or formula you can use to catapult your site to the top of search engine results. Using all the tactics that have been presented thus far won't absolutely guarantee best results, but at the very least, you will be following best practice guidelines, with the most valuable benefit of using these commands being the ability to somewhat control how your web page is described and listed in search results.

To check the effectiveness of the tags within your web page, there is an excellent FREE meta tag analyzer offered by Submit Express (www.submitexpress.com/analyzer). Use this tool to determine how you can further tweak, optimize, or revamp your site for better results. The tool allows you to see how search engine robots are analyzing your website (or your competitors' websites), get tips on how to improve your meta tags, check the keywords used on the page, find keyword density, and check the URLs and links found on the page.

USING KEYWORDS WITH GRAPHICS

Another great place for keywords is in the image descriptions found in graphics on a web page. In HTML, the <img> tag is used to embed, or place, an image on the page. Because spaces are not accepted within file names, hyphens are preferred. Here's an example:

```
<img src="graphics/online-book-marketing-cover.jpg" />
```

In the statement above, the "**src**" attribute stands for "source," and it supplies the name of the image while defining its location on the server relative to the current document. This image is called "online-book-marketing-cover.jpg" and can be found in the "graphics" folder.

Devising and creating descriptive file names like "black-volkswagen-golf.jpg" provides much more information to a search engine than an image named "IMG00023.jpg." Naming your graphic files this way also increases the chance that your images will show up in search results for engines such as Google Images, giving searchers yet another way to possibly run across your site.

The "**alt**" attribute can be (and should be) used along with the "**img**" tag. The information presented in the "**alt**" tag is indexed by search engines to also help determine a page's relevance for rankings. For a user, it provides alternative information for an image in the form of words displayed in place of a graphic if that graphic cannot be displayed for some reason. There are many reasons why a graphic may not be displayed:

- A user has his or her graphics turned off.
- There is a slow connection.
- An error appears within the "**src**" attribute code.
- The user is using a text-based browser such as those found on Unix and Linux systems.
- The user uses a screen reader, which is a talking browser for the visually impaired.

With that in mind, it's a good idea to combine your keyword phrase with an accurate description of your image, which should be no longer than five words maximum. An effective use of the "**alt**" attribute may be as follows:

<img src="graphics/online-book-marketing-cover.jpg" alt="Online book marketing front cover "/>

PLACING KEYWORDS IN TEXT LINKS

When the search engines come a-searchin', they also crawl and analyze the text links found on your site, so it is of utmost importance that these links also be relevant, descriptive, and contain your keyword phrases. Because text links stand out on a page, they are actually given higher priority and more weight than any surrounding text. Knowing this, you should never have worthless links that simply read "Click Here." Provide a clue as to what you're linking to with links that read "Click Here for (fill in the blank)," where the blank contains your relevant keywords.

PLACING KEYWORDS IN DOCUMENT TITLES AND URLS

When naming files, documents, and URLs, make sure to include keywords in the titles you create. Examples of good file names to use on our golf site might include the following:

Golf-swing-tips.htm
Golf-swing-instructions.htm
Golf-swing-training.htm
Improving-your-golf-swing-report.pdf
Improve-your-golf-instructional-video.mp4
Golf-tips-from-the-pros.mp3

KEYWORD DENSITY ANALYZER TOOLS

Now that you have a little HTML under your belt, we can further delve into keyword density analyzer tools. Sounds intimidating, but trust me, after you find out how much this will help you with keyword research and analyzing your own pages, you will merrily use these tools quite often. A keyword density analyzer tool allows you to measure the number of times your keyword phrase appears on a page relative to the total number of words found on that page.

The perfect balance in keyword density will optimize results and help you achieve higher search engine rankings. Remembering that keyword phrases should be no more than 7 percent of the total number of words presented on a page, here is a list of FREE keyword density analyzer tools you can use to check your web pages.

David Naylor (tools.davidnaylor.co.uk/keyworddensity)
Keyword Density (www.keyworddensity.com)
SEO Book (tools.seobook.com/general/keyword-density)

In the "Keyword Research Strategies" section on page 49, we used the tool found at ABAKUS Topword to look at the competition and analyze the most used single keywords, two-word phrases, and three-word phrases found on a page. The keyword density analyzer tool created by David Naylor (tools.davidnaylor.co.uk/keyworddensity) will allow you to take this research even further, giving you a list of all the keywords used within meta tags, graphic links, text links, and the "alt" descriptions found on a page. While visiting David Naylor's site, go through each of the summary tabs presented near the top of the page that read "Page," "Words," "Info," and "Links" to see various views of the information. I warned you that you would learn just enough to be dangerous, and I think it's now safe to say that you're officially there!

KEYWORD PLACEMENT SUMMARY

Let's summarize everything we have learned thus far. Without overstuffing our content with keyword phrases (which we can double-check using a keyword density analyzer tool), keywords should be placed in:

- The "title" tag
- The "description" meta tag
- The "keywords" meta tag
- The H1, H2, and H3 header tags
- The body text or content of your document
- The file names and URLs of documents and graphics
- The "alt" attribute used for graphic descriptions
- Link text

For "95 SEO Tips and Tricks for Powerful Search Engine Optimization," visit webdesign.about.com/od/seo/tp/seo_tips_and_tricks.01.htm. Notice the naming convention used for this document's URL! Hmm!

USING THE ROBOTS.TXT FILE AND "NOINDEX" META TAG

Although our aim is to create search engine friendly pages, there may be some files or directories you do not want to show up in search results and therefore don't want indexed at all. A "**robots.txt**" file is a simple text file (created in any text editor such as Notepad or TextEdit) that tells search engines not to crawl or index specified files or directories on your site. This file must be placed in the root (or top level) directory of your site.

On visiting a site, the first thing a bot does is look to see whether a robots.txt file exists. If this file does not exist or is not found, then the bot assumes there are no restrictions and proceeds to crawl and index the entire site. Let's look at the format of an example file:

User-agent: *
Disallow: /Graphics/
Disallow: /BusinessDocs/exclude-this.html

These statements in the robots.txt file tell all search engines (as indicated by the asterisk) not to index the Graphics directory as well as the "exclude-this.html" file found in the BusinessDocs folder. It is necessary to create a separate "Disallow" line for every file or directory that you wish to have excluded.

Although creating this file stops files from being indexed from within the site itself, pages may still be indexed and appear in search results if they are linked to from other sites on the Web. The only way to completely remove a page from results (whether linked to or not) is to use the "**noindex**" meta tag, which should be added along with the other meta tags that appear within the "**head**" section of the HTML document you wish to have excluded.

<meta name="robots" content="noindex, nofollow">

This statement disallows both indexing and the following of any links contained on the page. Statements like this one may be useful if there are unfinished pages you are still working on or if there are pages you create for your own personal use that would not necessarily be of value to your visitors. For more on the robots.txt file and the "noindex" meta tag, visit The Web Robots Pages (www.robotstxt.org).

Backlinks and SEO

Another factor to take into consideration when trying to up the ante in search results is the relationship you have with other websites on the Net and the number of backlinks (or inbound links) you receive from them. Search engines presume that if you have a lot of sites linking to you, then you must be providing valuable, resourceful content. In particular, Google's PageRank is one of the methods used to calculate the relevance and importance of a web page. Its algorithm interprets a link from page A to page B as a vote by page A for page B. It measures both the quantity AND quality (whether they come from reputable, important, high-ranking sites) of incoming links.

Don't be tempted to participate in any of the "1,000 Backlinks for $9.99" programs. You don't know where those links are from, what reputation the sites have, and whether or not any of them are blacklisted. Links from shady, questionable websites can negatively affect your rankings regardless of what other SEO techniques you employ.

In addition, search engines also check the relevancy of your inbound links. If your site's subject matter is basketball, it won't help you in the least to have a backlink from a dog grooming company's site, so stay away from backlink services where you have no control over who will be linked to your site. I advise that you concentrate on creating great content, and the rest will take care of itself. As we progress through this book, we will uncover numerous methods for generating quality backlinks to your site.

When adding outbound links to your site, make sure they highly relate to your website content and will further enhance your users' experience. To check the number of inbound and outbound links to your site, you can use Open Site Explorer (www.opensiteexplorer.org), which shows a detailed view of the page as well as the domain authority of incoming links. Use this tool to see what sites are linking to your competitors, as these will be sites that you can possibly pitch and market your book or site to as well.

Submitting Your Site to Search Engines and Directories

We have all seen the "We will submit your site to 75,000-plus search engines and directories for the low price of $29.95!" offers. But come on now…think about it. What 75,000 search engines and directories do you know of that exist? At most, I can recall about ten, and evidently they are the only ten I really need to know. So even if this claim is true, it is definitely overkill!

These days, search engines are so good at finding and indexing websites that it is no longer necessary for you to do the process yourself, whether by manual submission or through a paid service. For diehards and control freaks like me, and especially if you have a brand new site under a new domain, you should visit Free Web Submission (www.freewebsubmission.com), where you will find direct links to the top fifty highest ranked engines and directories that you can manually submit your site to. Hitting all fifty (once again, overkill) will have you in wonderful shape, but you really only need to submit to the following four:

Bing (www.bing.com/webmaster/SubmitSitePage.aspx)
Dmoz (www.dmoz.org)
Google (www.google.com/addurl)
Yahoo! (siteexplorer.search.yahoo.com/submit)

After you have submitted your site, check back periodically to see if it shows up in the results. It can take four to six weeks before it will show. If you have covered all the steps outlined in this chapter, you never know, your site may index significantly quicker.

Monitoring Your Website (or Blog)

After your site is up and running, and its coming up in search results, it's a good idea to check and analyze your web statistics to determine how users are interacting with your site. Most hosts include a basic, simple statistics package for FREE along with their hosting plans. FREE Google Analytics (www.google.com/analytics) is also a great and very popular tool that can be used to check site statistics and analyze incoming traffic.

Monitoring your site statistics will give you insight into what works on your site and what doesn't so that you might change the keywords you decided to use or improve your site design, content offerings, features, or functionality. Find out and monitor who visits your website, from where, when, what search terms are being used, how long they stay, what path they take, and on what pages they exit your site. Pay particular attention to the following statistics:

Keywords

This statistic monitors the keyword phrases visitors used to search for and find your site. Look at these results to determine whether your targeted words are accurate and effective or whether you need to update them. This statistic can also provide hints as to what additional content you may need to include on your site.

Unique or new visitors

This statistic lets you see how many different people visit your website within a fixed time frame, usually hourly, daily, weekly, or monthly. If the same visitor visits your site on January 1 and then again on January 3, then that visitor would be counted twice as a daily unique visitor and once as a weekly or monthly unique visitor.

Repeat visitors

If you are updating content regularly, then you can monitor the number of users who return again and again. If this number is reasonably high, then "Yea!" You are doing something right, and users are finding your content valuable.

Page views

This statistic shows which pages are the most popular on your site, indicating what readers are finding most valuable. This statistic can be used to see whether changes to certain pages result in more visits or what kind of content you need to provide to keep visitors satisfied.

Click path or visitor path

This statistic shows the actual path a visitor took while browsing through your website. For instance, you can see if they hit the main page and left after only viewing that page. Did you capture their interest where they looked at every page in your site before leaving? Or did they get halfway through and leave? Following this statistic can help you understand why visitors come to your site and what they look for when they get there.

Exit pages

This statistic shows the last page a reader visited before leaving your site. If you notice a high dropout rate on a certain page, then you may consider updating the content or simplifying the design. Although results are not conclusive, this statistic, used in conjunction with the click path or visitor path, may reveal what pages users find least useful, boring, or confusing.

Length of session

This statistic tells you how long the average visitor spent looking at your web pages. If you notice that visitors are not spending much time on certain pages, try to analyze why and assess what functionality or content you can add to increase the time spent there. On average, two to three minutes is a pretty good session length.

Web Tools and Resources

AddThis (www.addthis.com)

Create easy-to-use clickable buttons that allow users to share your website, blog, and newsletter information via Facebook, Twitter, Digg, StumbleUpon, email, and other means. AddThis also provides analytics that allow you to see exactly how and where your content is being shared.

Dimdim (www.dimdim.com)
Use Dimdim for FREE web meetings and collaborations. It offers video, voice, and phone conferencing through your desktop browser.

E-junkie (www.e-junkie.com)
This resource provides a shopping cart for selling downloads (ebooks, white papers, audio files, software, etc.) and tangible goods; it also allows for PayPal integration.

FreeConference (www.freeconference.com)
A FREE telephone conference call service

Google Analytics (www.google.com/analytics)
A powerful, flexible, and easy-to-use FREE web analytics solution that gives you insight into your website traffic, performance, and marketing effectiveness

Hivelogic's Enkoder (hivelogic.com/enkoder/app)
The FREE Enkoder for Mac OS X helps protect email addresses by converting them into encrypted JavaScript code so that only real people using real browsers can see them.

IE NetRenderer (ipinfo.info/netrenderer)
Allows you to check how a website looks in ALL versions of Internet Explorer to ensure universal compatibility

K7.net (voicemail.k7.net/signup)
A FREE fax to email service

KISSinsights (www.kissinsights.com)
Slide-in polls that give your customers a way to tell you what they need

phpBB (www.phpbb.com)
FREE open-source bulletin board/forum/chat room software. The package is also offered and available through most web hosts.

Picnik (www.picnik.com)
FREE, easy-to-use online photo editor that eliminates the need for Photoshop or other image editing tools.

SurveyMonkey (www.surveymonkey.com)
FREE power tool for creating web surveys

TwitThis (www.twitthis.com)
A button you can place in your HTML or blog code that allows readers to share what they're reading with followers on Twitter

Ustream (www.ustream.tv)
A FREE way to stream live video from your event

W3C Link Checker (validator.w3.org/checklink)
FREE service provided by the World Wide Web Consortium (W3C) that allows you to check for broken hyperlinks and orphaned pages throughout a website

W3C Markup Validation Service (validator.w3.org)
FREE service that helps check the validity of web documents to ensure that web page standards have been met

Website Grader (www.websitegrader.com)
A FREE diagnostic tool offered by HubSpot that measures the marketing effectiveness (or SEO) of any website

Xmarks (www.xmarks.com)
Sync your bookmarks across your computers and browsers for FREE. Xmarks seamlessly integrates with your web browser to keep your bookmarks safely backed up and in sync. Supports Firefox, Chrome, Internet Explorer, and Safari.

Zoomerang (www.zoomerang.com)
Tool to create FREE surveys online

Chapter 4:
Your Author Blog

The word *blog* is derived from "web log" and is in effect an online diary where you can publish your thoughts; share your views, ideas, and opinions; discuss issues; divulge information; give advice; report on breaking news; provide useful links, photos, and videos; or share your expertise and knowledge on a particular subject. As an interactive site, a blog can incorporate text, graphics, photos, videos, and other digital assets.

Blog posts are arranged in reverse chronological order, which means that when you visit a blog, the latest post will appear on the top, with older posts shown in descending order. A post includes a title, body text, optional graphics or video, a permalink (or permanent link, which is a URL that points to a specific blog post after it has passed from the front page into the archives), a comment link for readers' feedback, and a trackback link (see "Blogging and SEO" on page 72). A post sometimes includes a date and time stamp.

What has made blogs, blogging, and other social media tools so popular is that you can freely publish content to the Web with literally no technical knowledge necessary. As an author, the main purpose of your blog will be to promote and publicize your brand, book(s), and future projects, as well as get your name out there, create relationships, and establish yourself as a credible expert in your field. A blog allows you to easily attract new readers, and it helps in developing a loyal fan base so that you are not easily forgotten between releases.

> **Note:** According to a study performed by HubSpot (www.hubspot.com), websites with frequently updated blogs receive 55 percent more visitors, 97 percent more inbound links (which signals authority to search engines), and 434 percent more indexed pages than static websites that don't have a blog.

Things to Do with Your Blog

Here are some ideas for things you should do with your blog:

- Your blog's design and content should be consistent with your brand's message.
- You should incorporate a branded masthead that lets people know right away who you are and what your blog (and book) is all about.
- Promote your title by including a static "Buy the Book" page that features a picture of the cover, a short blurb or synopsis of the book, and a "Buy Now" button.
- On this "Buy the Book" page, feature a newsletter sign-up form that includes a free sample chapter (or other item of importance and relevance) upon subscription.
- Include an "About" page that should be used to let people know the reason for your blog's existence, what types of topics will be covered, and why you are qualified to write about these topics.
- Have a clearly marked "Contact" page that provides your contact details such as email and Skype.
- Incorporate links to your social media networking profiles.
- Aim to stay on topic and limit your blog posts to a well-defined niche.
- Keep posts brief, approximately 100 to 500 words per post.
- Post links to interesting articles, pictures, or videos and provide thought-provoking commentary.

- Focus on audience needs and wants. Poll your audience about what subjects they would like to see covered in the future.
- Never use blog posts to blatantly sell products.
- Use your blog to network with popular bloggers within your niche and courteously ask them to give your book a review.
- Update your blog a minimum of three times per week. Most popular bloggers update daily, if not several times per day.
- Publish original and unique content as opposed to syndicated content.
- Optimize posts for search engines (see the "Blogging and SEO" section on page 72).
- Make sure your blog accepts user comments, feedback, and reviews. (This technique can be used not only to engage your audience, but also to add more text to your blog, resulting in the site encompassing a much broader set of keywords that you may not have originally thought of or planned for.)
- Engage your readers by asking for feedback on any articles, posts, or topics. Literally add "What's your opinion?" "Do you agree?" or "What do you think?" to the end of your posts.
- Reply to reader comments to further extend the conversation. Remember to thank them for their posts and respect their views.
- Regularly police your site to remove any spam or offensive comments.
- Personalize your blog by showing how some of the information you present directly affects or relates to you. Share real life experiences that you or others have had with some of the subjects or topics that you write about.
- Humanize your blog by writing personal posts that have nothing to do with your subject every now and again. Let people know not only how smart you are, but that you are a real person, too. Be honest, be truthful, be you!
- Encourage audience participation by occasionally holding contests where you offer some type of prize giveaway.
- Increase the "stickiness" of your site by interlinking articles with a "Related Posts" section on each page.

- Include search capability.
- Provide visible, easy navigation for both old and related posts.
- Have clearly defined categories and subcategories so that visitors can easily hunt for–and find–other materials of interest.
- Keep your blog interesting by inviting guest bloggers from time to time. This strategy mixes it up a bit and provides fresh perspectives.

Tip: To aid in creating a successful blog, visit www.problogger.net/learn to purchase Darren Rowse's very popular and highly recommended ebook courses: *31 Days to Build a Better Blog* and *Copywriting Scorecard for Bloggers.* It's a purchase you won't regret!

Blogging and SEO

Search engines love blogs. Topic-specific, regularly updated blogs are rewarded by Google and other search engines with higher page rankings. As Rick Bruner, former research director of DoubleClick, put it, "Blog stands for Better Listings On Google." Frequently updated content means that spiders return regularly to reindex your content and ensure they always have the latest, most current information from your site. "The squeaky wheel gets the oil," as they say, so people searching for information on your particular topic will find you more quickly through a regularly updated blog than they would through a static website that does not have a blog or is not updated frequently. Always use carefully selected keywords for your title, body text, tags, and permalink (URL), as well as any graphics, audio and video file names, or link text you incorporate.

Another advantage a blog has over a static website is the ability to receive "trackbacks." A trackback is an automated alert that is sent to a blog owner to let him or her know that one of his or her blog posts has been linked to or referenced from another site. Most blogging software supports trackbacks. According to the settings of the particular platform, a trackback sends the name of the site that's referencing it, its URL, the title of the post, and a short excerpt of the contents. What's really great about this is that a trackback will automatically create a comment on the original post that was referenced; this comment provides a link to the new post, giving readers the opportunity to discover blogs within the same subject category, which can result in an increased amount of incoming traffic for the blogger who made the reference. Linking to or referencing relevant blog sites or posts within your niche can be used as a technique to get you noticed. It can also serve as a method for creating an abundance of inbound links. But don't abuse this trackback functionality. Make sure your readers are truly benefitting from the information that you link to.

Tip: For an easy way to generate links and get help with SEO, link the main keywords in your blog post to other relevant documents on your site at least once within the body text. Although internal linking is not as important as links from external sites, it still helps. When linking this way, make sure to use the full URL, including the "http://" part of the address.

Blogging Decisions

At this point in the game, you are presented with several options:

1. Should you have a website only?
2. Should you have a website that incorporates a blog?
3. Should you only have a blog?
4. Should you have a blog that is separate from your website?
5. Should you have neither?

I hope that no one has selected Option 5, considering the exposure and potential for book sales that can be derived from both a website and a blog. I cannot dictate which option will be best for you, as that will depend on your overall brand strategy. What long-term results do you want to accomplish with your online presence in addition to your short-term goal of selling books? Answering that will help you decide which option to choose. You have to pick the solution that works best for you.

I will say that the decision to create and maintain a blog should not be made lightly. Providing interesting, well-written content that is updated regularly to keep it fresh and exciting requires passion for your subject, commitment, self-discipline, self-motivation, and a considerable amount of time and effort. To develop a community, it will be necessary for you to interact regularly on the site by responding to readers, answering their questions, and thanking them for their comments and insights. You will learn the art of conversation as you learn to use reader-generated content (in the form of questions and comments) to further discussions in a way that makes other readers want to join in and get involved. Essentially, your blog is about asking your audience to participate in a two-way–I repeat, two-way–conversation with you.

If selecting Options 2, 3, or 4, then your next decision will be to choose which blogging platform or software you should use (presuming that you don't already have a blog in operation). Although there are numerous platforms to choose from, I suggest you start with either WordPress (www.wordpress.org) or TypePad (www.typepad.com).

With over twenty million installations of the software worldwide, WordPress is rated the number one blogging software on the Web. It is freely available for download, or if you already have a web host (as the software requires installation on a web server), it can easily be installed through a tool called Fantastico. Just check with your host for details. It is literally a one-click set up process.

Note: For help with WordPress installations, I highly recommend Ken Dawes, "The Web Mechanic." Find him at www.the-web-mechanic.com.

The reason for WordPress's number one rating is because of the unlimited number of add-ons, plug-ins, themes, tools, and features available, giving you the flexibility to grow your blog any which way you may need to in the future. Depending on your specifications and feature requirements, if not technically inclined, you may need to hire a developer (see Ken above) who can brand the site with an appropriate theme and install the various plug-ins you need. After the initial setup and customization is complete, posting will be a breeze. Choosing this option allows you to either have a stand-alone blog or incorporate your blog into your existing site. Either way, you will need your own domain name and a hosting plan to implement this solution.

Tip: For a list of "Essential WordPress Plug-ins," as recommended by Ken Dawes, please see Appendix B on page 187.

TypePad has the ability to host your blog, so there is no need for you to have a domain name or additional hosting plan. This option is not free, however, and plans run from $8.95 to $29.95 per month, with a 14-day FREE trial. It's a quick and easy, no-fuss solution, with hundreds of themes and layouts available that you can put together through the use of a simple, drag-and-drop interface. You can upload a custom banner and use HTML, CSS, and JavaScript for additional customization.

With TypePad, you have the ability to map your domain name. Otherwise, your address will end up being yourblogname.typepad.com, something that as professional branders, we would never do. You also have the ability to add permanent pages (like the "About" or "Contact" pages from a regular site) that can match your blog's theme. This option allows you to have a stand-alone blog or create a kind of hybrid solution that incorporates both a blog along with static pages. There are widgets for Twitter, LinkedIn, PayPal, and Amazon, so if you need to link to your book on Amazon, you can. The service automatically feeds your content to search engines, blocks spam that can appear in comments, and provides blog traffic statistics. Lastly, WordPress and TypePad both have applications that let you blog directly from your mobile device.

Note: For the offenders who picked Option 5 on page 73, FiledBy (www. filedby .com) offers you an alternative solution for an author's platform and has a premium plan for $99 per year that incorporates, you guessed it, an author blog. Check them out for more details!

Before you start on your blogging journey, it is a good idea to seek out other blogs in and outside of your industry to see how it's already being done and to find out what you could do that's either different or better. Become a part of some of these communities and start commenting and getting involved. Here is a list of directories that will help you with your blog search. Most people are partial to Technorati with regards to this type of information.

Best of the Web Blogs (blogs.botw.org)
Bloggers (bloggers.com)
EatonWeb (portal.eatonweb.com)
Google Blog Search (blogsearch.google.com)
IceRocket (blogs.icerocket.com)
Technorati (technorati.com/blogs/directory)

Tip: For *Advertising Age*'s daily rankings of the Power 150 marketing blogs, visit http://adage.com/power150/.

Finding Blog Topics

To be a good blogger, you really have to enjoy reading, researching, and communicating on the Net because this is how you'll find information that will be of interest, as well as value, to your readers. It's a good idea to keep a list of topics you could possibly blog about in case you get stuck for ideas or inspiration later on down the line. When searching for topics, look for recurring themes. What types of questions are being asked over and over again? Use your blog to answer those questions, and if visiting online forums (a blogger's gold mine), then you'll have the opportunity to post a link back to your blog with the answer to the question at hand.

Visit other blogs within your niche. Check which ones have large followings, so you can find out best practices. Look at the content. What topics solicit the most responses? Is there a way to revise or update a story? Can you come up with a completely different angle or perspective? How about expounding on an idea already presented? Or totally disagreeing with another?

Write quick and easy bullet-point lists (e.g., "The Top 10 Ways to…"). People also love how-tos. You've seen this one a thousand times: "How to Get the Man (or Woman) of Your Dreams." Conduct interviews and provide Q&A articles. Compile a profile of someone who is either very knowledgeable (an expert) or is up and coming in your field. Find out the latest industry news, gossip, and trends. Provide a book, product, service, or website review that pertains to your field. Basically, you just have to be creative and keep your ear to the ground. Find out what people are into or curious about, what they like or dislike. Content is all around you; you just have to look for it.

Also, be aware that people love pictures, so you should consider spicing up your posts with some type of graphic imagery. As a former editorial director, I used to make sure that readers knew exactly what the story was about from only reading the headline and looking at the accompanying graphic(s). You should consider doing the same with your blog. To get content ideas and images for your blog, check the following resources.

SITES FOR CONTENT IDEAS

Alexa (www.alexa.com)
Alexa, a subsidiary of Amazon, is known as the web information company that computes traffic rankings provided by the millions of Alexa toolbar users in order to provide you with the top 500 sites on the Web.

Alltop (www.alltop.com)
Alltop collects the headlines of the latest stories from the best websites and blogs that cover a specific topic. It then groups these collections

–"aggregations"– into individual web pages and displays the five most recent headlines from these information sources. Topics run from adoption to zoology, with stories about photography, food, science, religion, celebrities, fashion, gaming, sports, politics, automobiles, Macintosh, and hundreds of other subjects in between.

BuzzFeed (www.buzzfeed.com)
BuzzFeed tracks the Web's obsessions in real time.

Digg (www.digg.com)
Digg is a place for people to discover and share content from anywhere on the Web, covering the latest headlines, videos, and images.

Engadget (www.engadget.com)
Engadget is a web magazine with daily coverage of everything new in gadgets and consumer electronics.

Google Alerts (www.google.com/alerts)
These are weekly, daily, or instantaneous alerts, sent to you via email, that contain the latest, most relevant Google results based on your choice of keywords or topics. Basically, it's an automatic news finder!

Google News (news.google.com)
Google News is a computer-generated news site that aggregates headlines from more than 4,500 English-language news sources worldwide. Similar stories are then grouped together and displayed according to personalized interests.

Google Trends (www.google.com/trends/hottrends)
Up-to-the-minute information on the hottest searches in the United States.

Mashable (www.mashable.com)
Mashable provides social media news and web tips.

Newsvine (www.newsvine.com)
Owned by MSNBC Interactive News (msnbc.com), Newsvine's purpose is "to build a perfectly different, perfectly efficient way to read, write, and interact with the news." Read stories from established media organizations as well as individual contributors from around the world.

popurls (www.popurls.com)
Known as the dashboard for the latest web buzz, it's a single page that encapsulates up-to-the-minute headlines from the most popular sites on the Internet.

reddit (www.reddit.com)
Touted as the voice of the Internet, it's like news before it happens.

Stuff To Tweet (www.stufftotweet.com)
It features the hottest topics as found on Digg, Delicious, Twitter, YouTube, Lifehacker, TMZ, Mashable, wikiHow, CNN, *New York Times*, Dailymotion, Amazon, and craigslist.

StumbleUpon (www.stumbleupon.com)
StumbleUpon helps you discover and share great websites, delivering high-quality pages that are matched to your personal preferences.

TechCrunch (www.techcrunch.com)
A media blog that profiles start-ups, reviews new Internet products, and reports on breaking tech news.

Techmeme (www.techmeme.com)
A single, easy-to-scan page that contains all the must-read tech stories.

Technorati (www.technorati.com)
Technorati is a blog directory covering numerous subjects and

categories that also gives you the top 100 blogs of the day (www.technorati.com/blogs/top100/).

Trendwatching.com (www.trendwatching.com)
This site features emerging consumer trends, insights, and related hands-on business ideas from around the world.

SITES FOR FREE GRAPHICS AND IMAGES

Flickr (www.flickr.com/creativecommons)
You can use these FREE images in exchange for attribution.

FreeFoto.com (www.freefoto.com)
Here you'll find pictures you can use for FREE.

FreePhotosBank (www.freephotosbank.com)
Stock photos and images available for FREE.

morgueFile (www.morguefile.com)
This site offers FREE photos for creatives by creatives.

PhotoXpress (www.photoxpress.com)
Receive up to ten FREE stock photos per day upon registration.

Ideas for Blog Promotion

Here are a few ideas you can use to promote your blog:

- Incorporate both RSS and email subscription capability, as some people have no idea what RSS is all about (see "Understanding RSS" on page 82).

- Include social media sharing buttons (Facebook, Twitter, and others) to make it easy for readers to share your content.
- Announce your best blog posts via email and on Facebook, Twitter, or other social networking sites. If posting to Twitter, use the hashtag symbol as it relates to your subject (e.g., #golfswingtips).
- Search for questions on Twitter and LinkedIn that relate to your particular subject and respond by presenting a link to a relevant blog post you created.
- Participate in other communities. Visit relevant forums, groups, and blogs to leave feedback or answer questions, leaving links to your blog or a relevant blog post that relates to the question at hand.
- Network and build relationships with other bloggers in your field. After a relationship is established, ask for links to your relevant posts.
- Interview popular, respected bloggers as a way to increase awareness.
- Widen your audience by guest posting on blogs for bloggers who need to take a breather. Always include a link back to your blog in the byline.
- Include a blogroll, which is technospeak for a sidebar menu of your favorite blogs that you recommend. Blogrolls can be great traffic generators, as it is common for bloggers to reciprocate and add you to their blogroll list in turn. Increase your chances for reciprocation by making sure your blog is alive, kicking, and in full swing.
- Find out which sites are sending you the most traffic and consider building relationships with them.
- Find out who is linking to the popular blogs in your subject category by going to Google and typing in "link:www.the_blogs_url.com." Use the list to generate inbound links by promoting your blog's content to these sites using the methods discussed thus far.
- Bookmark and tag your best posts at sites like Digg (www.digg.com), Delicious (www.delicious.com), StumbleUpon (www.stumbleupon.com), and reddit (www.reddit.com).
- Submit new posts to search engines and directories (see "Ping Your Blog" on page 84).

- Add your blog's URL to your email signature, business cards, website (if separate), press kit, press releases, brochures, flyers, bookmarks, and any other promotional materials you have.

Note: I do not advise syndicating your blog content across all social networks and announcing every single blog post, as people who follow you on multiple networks may view this behavior as somewhat "spammy." Instead, I suggest you only post your best, most relevant posts to other networks.

Understanding RSS

RSS (also known as an Atom feed) stands for "Really Simple Syndication," and it allows you to syndicate or distribute content or a summary of content to a subscriber who is automatically (and almost instantaneously) notified every time you add new content to your blog, website, or podcast series. The information is delivered directly to subscribers without the need to bypass any filters (as is the case with email marketing) and is displayed through an RSS reader, also known as a "news aggregator" for text and a "podcatcher" for podcasts. RSS readers can be web-based, desktop-based, or mobile-device-based.

The most popular RSS readers can be found at Google Reader (www.google.com/reader) and through My Yahoo!. The latest versions of Internet Explorer and Safari have readers built in, as does Firefox, that incorporate a live bookmarks feature. RSS readers function somewhat like email with the list of unread feeds, or headings, from the different subscribed-to websites (or resources) aggregately displayed in one place. When you click an entry, you can see, read, or hear the latest updates from right there within the feed, or you can choose to click through to the particular site.

Give interested visitors a way to subscribe, stay updated, and become loyal readers without the need to even have to physically visit your site. By syndicating your content, you will generate a ton of backlinks to your site, and we all know how much search engines just love backlinks. Having an

RSS feed also increases your blog's visibility because now you can send your content directly to news aggregators like Yahoo! and Google. Sites that offer subscriptions have a little RSS or XML icon (usually orange in color) placed somewhere on the page. An RSS icon may also be displayed to the right of a URL in the browser window's address bar. To subscribe to a feed, simply click on the icon and follow the instructions that are presented on-screen.

RSS TOOLS

As most blogging software automatically creates an RSS feed for you, all you may need to do is turn the option on and forget about it. If your software does not provide this automatic RSS function, then you can try one of the services listed below. I have also included Feed Validator so you can ensure that your RSS output (or XML code) has been generated without errors.

FeedBlitz (www.feedblitz.com)
This is an email marketing service for blogs, social media, and RSS.

FeedForAll (www.feedforall.com)
Easily create, edit, and publish RSS feeds and podcasts (including iTunes-compatible podcasts) with desktop software. Available for Mac.

Feed Validator (www.feedvalidator.org)
This ensures that there are no problems with your feed. Any errors found will be highlighted, and the appropriate message will be given.

Google FeedBurner (www.feedburner.com)
This online feed creation and management service is compatible with several popular blog engines and provides statistical information, such as how many subscribers you have and what articles are most popular

on your site. Feed updates can be automatically delivered by web portal, newsreader, or email.

Jitbit RSS Feed Creator (www.jitbit.com/rss-feed-creator)
This RSS feed editor software tool lets you create, edit, and publish feeds and podcasts. Available for Windows.

Twitterfeed (www.twitterfeed.com)
Twitterfeed feeds your blog directly to Twitter, Facebook, and various other platforms.

PING YOUR BLOG

After you have RSS set up and you are regularly updating your site, then it will be necessary for you to ping your blog. Pinging your blog allows you to immediately notify blog search engines, directories, and other services every time new and updated content appears on your site. When a site receives your ping, in the form of your blog's URL, it enters a queue for indexing and addition to the site. Although most blogging software, like WordPress and TypePad, automatically pings a selected set of services, you may want to take an extra few minutes to help improve visibility and the speed at which search engines will index your blog by performing a manual ping using one or two of the FREE services below. Ping-O-Matic is the most popular.

Autopinger (www.autopinger.com)
BlogBuzzer (www.blogbuzzer.com)
Feed Shark (feedshark.brainbliss.com)
Google Blog Search Ping Service (blogsearch.google.com/ping)
Pingates (www.pingates.com)
Ping-O-Matic (www.pingomatic.com)

Measuring Your Blog's Success

Everybody will have different criteria, according to their desired goals, for measuring a blog's success. Use the statistics package that comes installed on your blog, or you can use the Google Analytics service, to identify and understand your main sources of traffic and the keywords used to search for and find your blog. With this information you can decide what activities you need to continue focusing on, increase, or possibly even eliminate completely.

Like all other mediums, you cannot expect your blog to be an overnight success. But armed with a commitment for the long haul and always looking for ways to refine what works and what doesn't, over time you should see the results you desire. A blog's success can be measured by any of the following:

- The number of visits
- The number of visitors
- The number of new visitors versus the number of returning visitors
- The number of page views per visit
- How long visitors stay engaged on the site
- The number of comments received
- The quality of comments received
- The general feedback received
- How many people are citing and linking your blog
- The number of "shares" you receive from your visitors to their social networks
- The number of RSS or email subscriptions
- The number of newsletter sign-ups
- Search engine rankings
- The number of book sales that resulted from your blogging activities. (Note that if you are performing numerous online marketing activities, then the results from one particular effort can be hard to determine or track without the use of a specific URL or code.)

PART III

Social Media Marketing

Chapter 5: Twitter

Ah, Twitter, my favorite online tool of choice! Twitter is a microblogging platform where you send out messages (called tweets) that consist of up to 140 characters. Even though you're an author, you'll soon become more adept at using the English language after you start tweeting. It's a real-time tool that allows you to connect on a personal level with readers, friends, fans, celebrities, professionals, organizations, and others who share similar interests. Twitter is based on the premise that you use your outgoing messages to answer the question of "What's happening?" but those 140 characters can be used for so much more. Twitter can be used to:

- Further enhance your personal brand
- Find your target audience of potential readers and customers
- Inform followers of upcoming book releases and promotions
- Hold contests and give away free prizes, such as autographed copies of your book
- Share awards, reviews, testimonials, or any other type of industry recognition you receive
- Notify followers of upcoming events, appearances, interviews, seminars, and classes
- Request book reviews and referrals

- Respond to questions and give advice in your area of expertise
- Let people know about new blog posts, podcasts, videos, articles, and press releases
- Poll your audience for opinions, ideas, help, advice, feedback, and answers to questions
- Announce breaking news in and outside of your industry
- Discover emerging trends within your industry
- Meet and converse one-on-one with other authors, readers, writers, editors, agents, publishers, and marketers
- Follow experts, competitors, and industry leaders
- Find experts you may wish to interview or invite to be guest bloggers and speakers
- Give or receive live coverage of events as they happen
- Share links to interesting sites, articles, blogs, videos, pictures, topics, and resources
- Share personal information as to what you're doing, why you're doing it, how you're feeling, or what you're going through
- Provide opinions, ideas, or random thoughts you may have
- Share jokes or inspirational messages and quotes (a Twitter favorite)
- Set up meetings (called Tweetups) with other users in your area
- Give book, movie, product, and service reviews or recommendations
- Land jobs, freelance gigs, or speaking and teaching engagements
- Announce job openings, hire help, or research prospects. (You can learn a lot about a person on Twitter.)
- Get customer service or learn about promotional deals from companies like Starbucks, Whole Foods Market, The Home Depot, Dunkin' Donuts, and many more
- Share other people's tweets that you find most useful or interesting (called retweeting)
- Recommend to your network other tweeps (Twitter people) to follow

These are just a few of the many ways Twitter can be used. If you imagine that everyone else is doing the things listed above and more, then it makes Twitter an ultratrendy, super cool place to hang out. Now that you know what Twitter's all about and what it can be used for, let's get down to business.

Setting Up Your Profile

Your first order of business is to head over to Twitter (www.twitter.com) and create an account. Here are the steps involved.

Step 1: Sign Up

Hit the "Sign Up" button and enter the following:

Full Name: People may use this field to search for you, so keep it personal and use your real name or pen name. The name you list here will appear above the bio presented on your home page.

Username: This is your Twitter "handle" or login. It can be up to fifteen characters in length and has to be unique, as the URL to your Twitter home page will become http://twitter.com/#!/yourusername (where "yourusername" is whatever you decide to select). Here are some examples of usernames you may recognize: @lorraine_phill, @BarackObama, @Ladygaga, @Oprah, @TheEllenShow, @stevejobs, @iamdiddy, and @tonyrobbins. As quoted from Mashable (@mashable), "You can't truly own your personal brand if you don't even own your Twitter handle." Choose a name that's in line with your brand, using your full name, domain, or a close variation. Whichever way you decide to go, much like selecting a domain, make sure it's catchy as well as easy to spell, pronounce, and remember. Although you can change your name later, it is advisable that you don't, as it will cause confusion for those who are already following you. Have a good think about it. Then choose a name you can ultimately stick with.

Lastly, enter your Password and Email Address. (Be sure to check the box under your email address if you would like people to be able to find you by this address.) Your email won't be listed on the site or be viewable by Twitter users; it will only be used for communications that come directly from Twitter itself. After you've completed the sign-up process, you can expect to receive a confirmation email.

The next set of pages in the sign-up process allows you to start following Twitter users. You can search by name, topic, or industry. Just hit the plus button to start following a user, which means that person's tweets will now show up on your home page in what is called your "timeline." You will also be presented with the ability to import and follow friends or contacts from other services such as Yahoo!, LinkedIn, Gmail, and Hotmail. Although you might want to go ahead and jump in, I suggest you hold off until you finish setting up your profile, which includes your bio information, before you do. That way, people will know who you are and what you are about before they decide to follow you back, which is the primary way of getting followers. If there is no information about you on your page, then it is highly unlikely that someone will choose to follow you back–that would be like following Mr. or Mrs. Nobody!

Step 2: Set up your profile (Settings > Profile)

The FIRST thing to do is upload a picture of yourself. The maximum size is 700 kilobytes, and files can be either JPG, GIF, or PNG formats. Don't use your book cover, logo, pet, favorite vacation spot, or a picture of the kids. I'm not being inhumane, but this is about *personal* branding. Keep it personal by providing a tight headshot, without a busy background, that shows you looking relaxed, professional, and approachable. Your picture should help people get a feel for who you are and what your personality might be like. I've received numerous comments on my apparently "dazzling" smile, which goes to show that a good picture can make all the difference. Aim to use the same picture across all social networks, so it is easier for people to find and recognize you both online and offline.

Enter your actual location into the searchable location box, whether it be Buffalo, New York, or Venice, Italy. "Earth," "The World," "The Universe," "All Over," or "Everywhere" are just not good descriptions for a location. Putting your actual location can be advantageous in case someone wants to invite you to an event, hire you as a guest speaker, work on a collaboration, meet for a coffee, or something of that nature. When people know your location, then they'll have an idea whether they need to fly you in, contact you by Skype, or use some other means to engage you. I must admit I was previously an offender. Being an international traveler, I started off my account with "The World" as my location because that's just the way it feels sometimes, but I soon got wise and decided to go with my base location of Atlanta, Georgia.

Next, enter your website or blog address into the website field. Lastly, fill out your bio. Your bio is extremely important as people find out all about you in 160 characters or fewer. Target your bio to your ideal reader. Make it interesting. With so few characters to describe yourself, you have no excuse but to do so. The description you provide should also give some type of clue as to what you might possibly be tweeting about.

When looking for people to follow, it is possible to search a bio for certain words or phrases. Make sure you have "author," "writer," or whatever word(s) you feel describe yourself in your bio so that you can be easily found, whether by other authors, agents, publishers, booksellers, or readers. The last two books I purchased and read were by authors I had never heard of before, but had discovered through Twitter.

Step 3: Create a custom background (Settings > Design)

Because we are building a brand that should remain relatively consistent across mediums, it is not acceptable to use the default Twitter background or the standard selection of background themes that are available. Creating a brand means you look different from everyone else, and that's what you will have to do here. Twitter has provided the means for us to brand ourselves, and any smart brander is going to make use of that real estate.

Use the space to get creative and show off your brand's personality. To upload your design after you have created a customized background, go to Settings > Design > Change background image. Having an attractive Twitter background (and tweeting great content) can help boost the number of followers you receive. Review other users' pages to get ideas for how you'd like your background to look.

Figure 3: Change Background Image Button

Tip: For an excellent gallery of Twitter backgrounds, see www.twitterbackgroundsgallery.com.

When deciding on a design for the background of my Twitter account (@lorraine_phill), I decided to put a funky, vibrant graphic on the left (as Westerners read from left to right) and a list of the books I've written and products I've created on the right. I chose to make the page about me first–who I am, the things I like, what I'm into–and about my books second. You can choose to do it the other way around or in a completely different way. It just depends on how you wish to present yourself and your brand.

If you previously used a designer to create your website or blog, then call that designer up and let him or her know you need to have a customized Twitter background made. You can also choose to hire a freelancer. Don't think of creating your background as too small a job to get it done that way; just get the job done professionally any which way you can.

Tip 1: If you dabble in graphic design and know how to use software such as Photoshop, you can find a tutorial on how to create a Twitter background at www.twitip.com/custom-twitter-backgrounds.

Tip 2: For professionally designed custom Twitter backgrounds priced at $99, check www.custombackgroundsfortwitter.com.

Tip 3: For a FREE intermediary solution, check Twitpaper (www.twitpaper.com) or TwitBacks (www.twitbacks.com).

Things You Should Know

It was quite embarrassing, as an IT professional and former programmer, to discover that Twitter had me completely stumped for a few weeks. I read and read but just could not get the hang of it until I finally had that "Aha" moment. Twitter is one of those tools you just have to use before you actually get it, so don't feel intimidated just yet. Here are a few things you need to know before you get your feet wet. Or should I say, before you take the plunge?

Your Tweets

Your tweets are publicly visible by default, meaning they can be read by anyone in the world, not just by other Twitter users. When someone decides to follow you, your tweets will show up in real time on their timeline. You can protect or lock your tweets (Settings > Account > Tweet Privacy) so that they'll no longer be visible to the public, and only the people you manually approve will be able to read them. Protecting your tweets, however, sort of defeats the purpose of creating an online brand. Your personal brand is supposed to make it easy for people to find, contact, connect, or learn more about and from you, so it makes no sense to lock your tweets down unless you're wanted by the Feds.

Direct Messages (DMs)

On Twitter, you have a messages inbox that functions somewhat like an email inbox where users can send you Direct Messages, or DMs, of 140 characters or fewer. To access your inbox, hit the "Messages" button that appears on the top pane. Messages sent to this inbox are completely private (not public) and only viewable by you. You can send private messages to other Twitter users, but the only catch is that they have to be following you. You can send a direct message by preceding a tweet with the letter "D," so the format would be "D @lorraine_phill your message." (Note the space before the @ symbol.) Because it's a private message, it won't show up on your timeline (or mine) for others to read; instead I will receive the direct message in my inbox. The other way to send a DM is if you are in your own inbox and click on a message from a user that appears in the left pane. Here, you can use the input box at the top of the right pane to send a DM back to that user. Lastly, you can send a message directly from a user's page by simply hitting the "Message" button above his or her timeline, which only appears if that particular user is actually following you.

Note: Go to Settings > Notices to change your settings to be notified by email every time you receive either a DM or a new follower on Twitter.

Auto DMs

When using a desktop client, which allows you to use Twitter from your desktop instead of through a browser window (see "Tools You Might Need" on page 99), it is possible to set up a standardized automatic DM that goes out to new followers instantaneously. Some users consider these messages to be spam and don't appreciate receiving them, but in my experience, that has been less than 1 percent of all users. Please don't tout your book here. Instead, use your auto DM to thank users for the follow and possibly (you didn't hear it from me) give them information on additional social networks where they can also connect with you.

Using the At (@) Sign

If you wrote a tweet that read, "@lorraine_phill loved the new book," this would indicate that your tweet was specifically directed at me. The way I would see the message (which shows publicly in your timeline) is if I click on the "@Mentions" tab on my home page. This tab provides me with a list of all the people who have mentioned @lorraine_phill in their tweets. I could then reply, "@yourname thanks so much." This is what makes Twitter a powerful open communications tool. We don't even have to be following each other to communicate this way. You have the power to talk to absolutely anybody out there, so use this power wisely.

Retweeting (RT)

If you're reading someone's timeline and you come across a tweet you'd like to share with your followers, then simply hit the "Retweet" link that appears on the message itself, and that message will appear as part of YOUR timeline as well as in your followers' timelines. Your followers will see that you've taken the time to highlight a user who provided a great message, and they may decide to check that user out. After visiting the user's page and seeing that he or she provides valuable tweets, your followers may decide to follow the user you retweeted. Let's flip the script. You provide a tweet of value. Someone reads it and thinks it may be of interest to his or her followers, so decides to retweet your tweet. Now you've been exposed to a whole bunch of users who may decide to follow you after visiting your page; reading your bio; and seeing your fantastic, professionally designed background as well as your super friendly, inviting pic. That's the value of providing great tweets and one of the ways to build a following. Are you beginning to see how this whole thing fits together?

> **Note:** You do not have to be following someone in order to retweet his or her tweets. You can check to see which of your tweets have been retweeted under the "Retweets" tab on your home page.

Using the Hashtag (#) Symbol

Hashtags present yet another way for users to find you. Using the hashtag in front of a subject or term allows you to categorize your tweets in a way that makes them searchable and, more importantly, findable on Twitter. For instance, if your area of expertise is social media marketing, you may want to end your tweets that are relevant to the subject with "#smm." Anyone who is interested in that subject can do a Twitter search for #smm and pull up all the relevant tweets and information from people who they may not already follow and would not otherwise have found. The search is in real time, so don't expect your tweets from last week to show up in results. Hashtags have been used for a variety of reasons, including breaking news, providing live feedback from events, and communicating during natural disasters. A popular hashtag is #followfriday. Every Friday people provide recommendations to their followers of other Twitterers to follow. If you wanted to participate (on a Friday of course), then your tweet would read something like "#followfriday @lorraine_phill @mashable" until you hit your 140-character limit. You can create your own original hashtag for a particular purpose. I created #obm for online book marketing discussions. Visit Tagdef (www.tagdef.com) for a hashtag directory. You can also view trending hashtag topics in the right-hand pane of your home page.

Going Mobile

If you're on the move, you can go to Settings > Mobile and change your settings to allow you to send tweets and to receive notices of direct messages, @Mentions, and tweets from people you've enabled for mobile notifications via text message on your phone.

Tip: Stay updated on the latest Twitter developments by following Twitter's official blog at http://blog.twitter.com.

Tools You Might Need

There are about a trillion tools and third-party applications that have been developed for Twitter. Here are a few of the ones that I find to be the most useful.

URL Shorteners

You'll soon be sharing links to interesting articles, blog posts, videos, and pictures you find on the Net. Google URL Shortener (goo.gl) and bitly (bit.ly) shorten lengthy URLs to make it easier for you to stay within the 140-character limit. Both services provide click statistics, too.

Picture Sharing Service

You may wish to share interesting photos or graphics along with your tweets. TwitPic (www.twitpic.com) lets you post photos to Twitter from either your phone, their website, or via email.

Music Sharing Service

You can share music and podcasts with MP3 Twit (www.mp3twit.com).

Apps for Your Phone or Mobile Device

A better alternative to text messaging your Tweets is to use an app. If you have a smartphone that has Wi-Fi or 3G access (who doesn't nowadays?), there's a whole host of Twitter apps available for download. This list will get you started.

Android – Twidroyd (www.twidroyd.com)
Blackberry – UberSocial (www.ubersocial.com)
iPhone, iPad, and iPod touch – HootSuite for Twitter (available for FREE from the iTunes App Store; allows you to manage both your Twitter and Facebook accounts)
Windows Mobile – Twitter (comes preinstalled)

Desktop Clients Available in Mac OS X and Windows Formats

These applications allow you to access Twitter directly from your desktop without the need to open a browser window. They provide added functionality, such as the ability to view your timeline, DMs, @Mentions, and searches all at once from one screen; built-in URL shorteners; instant notifications of messages; and the ability to cross-post your updates to other sites like Facebook and LinkedIn.

Seesmic (www.seesmic.com/seesmic_desktop/sd2)
Twhirl (www.twhirl.org)
TweetDeck (www.tweetdeck.com)

Web Apps for Twitter

These apps let you further extend Twitter's functionality and update posts across a variety of social media accounts.

HootSuite (www.hootsuite.com)
Includes the ability to manage and post to multiple networks (Facebook, LinkedIn, and your blog), schedule posts, upload images, manage multiple users over various social network accounts, and track statistics

Ping.fm (ping.fm)
Allows you to update ALL your social networks in a snap

SocialOomph (www.socialoomph.com)
Includes the ability to schedule tweets, send automatic DMs to new followers, view @Mentions and retweets, and track keywords

Other Recommended Tools

Friend or Follow (www.friendorfollow.com)
Allows you to find out who's not following you back, who you're not following back, and who your mutual friends are

Monitter (monitter.com)
Real-time tool that lets you monitor Twitter for a selected set of keywords. Use it to find out what people are saying about you, your book, or your industry.

Topify (www.topify.com)
This email notification system provides detailed information on new followers and offers you the ability to follow back, reply, unfollow, or block a user from within the email itself.

Tweetake (www.tweetake.com)
Completely back up your tweets and lists with Tweetake.

TweetBeep (www.tweetbeep.com)
Keep track of conversations that mention you, your book, your website, or your blog with hourly updates via email.

Twitoria (www.twitoria.com)
Twitoria finds your friends who haven't tweeted in a while so that you can decide whether to keep following them or not.

Twitter Counter (www.twittercounter.com)
Get stats, graphs, and widgets for–and of–your Twitter account.

TweetEffect (www.tweeteffect.com)
Find out which of your Twitter updates made people either follow or leave you.

Twitterfeed (www.twitterfeed.com)
Feed your blog to Twitter, Facebook, or other platforms.

Tweet Reminder (www.tweetreminder.com)
Tweet Reminder keeps track of all your important diary dates via your Twitter account and sends you a DM on the date that you set so that you never forget a special event.

Twitter Resources (twitter.com/about/resources)
Official Twitter resource offering widgets, logos, icons, as well as tweet share and follow buttons.

Wildfire Promotion Builder (wildfireapp.com)
This easy-to-use software allows you to incorporate branded interactive campaigns, such as sweepstakes, quizzes, contests, coupons, giveaways, and incentive-based surveys. Branded campaigns can be simultaneously published to both Facebook and Twitter.

Tweeting on Twitter

Now you are finally ready to tweet! Before you start following en masse, it's a good idea to go ahead and get your timeline going. I must admit I was initially struck by stage fright. I mean, what should I say? Who would even care? Thoughts of doom lurked in my mind. I think the problem was that being a multidimensional being, I just didn't know where to start, but eventually I did, and as the saying goes, the rest is history. It will be the same for you. Think about the brand you are attempting to convey. Then find a way to personalize it. You probably won't come out with your bat swinging right away, but after a couple attempts, you'll get the hang of it. And if all else fails, there is always the delete key, so no harm can be done.

Don't use Twitter solely for the purpose of promoting your title, although you'll be doing that in a roundabout way. Occasional plugs are okay, but make sure to keep them few and far between. I mean, how many tweets can you put out regarding your book before your timeline becomes redundant, uninteresting, repetitive, predictable, and just plain boring. You can't expect to gain followers that way. Your focus should be on building relationships, and the way to help do that is by providing useful, interesting, educational, and inspirational tweets.

It's also a good idea to not have too much of one "thing" in your timeline. Show your activity on the network by mixing up original tweets, retweets, and @Mentions. Don't have huge marathons of @Mentions in your timeline. Pages of @Mentions make your timeline look boring and can indicate to potential followers that you are caught up in a bunch of microconversations with people you already know and therefore probably won't have much time to interact with them. Be inviting and break up your @Mentions with plenty of original tweets between.

There is always the debatable question of frequency. You'll have to make that determination yourself, but the unofficial rule is between two and five tweets per day. People want to see you tweeting daily and probably won't follow you (or will unfollow you) if they see huge gaps within your timeline, with weeks or months between tweets. Remember, this service is about actively participating in the conversation.

Finding Followers

Twitter is the ultimate two-way communications networking tool that allows you to build beneficial connections (as well as make friends) in and outside of your industry. You can follow absolutely anybody you would like to on the network, as there's no need for anyone to accept or approve of you following them, unless that person's tweets are protected. You can't expect followers if you're not following anyone, and there are hosts of directories and tools that can help you find people to follow.

To cut down on aggressive following behaviors and spamming activities, Twitter imposes certain restrictions that limit the number of users you can follow based on the number of followers you already have. The restrictions kick in after you are following over 2,000 users. As Twitter puts it, you can't follow 10,000 people if only 100 are following you. On the flip side, there is no limit to the number of followers you can have following you.

Initially, you'll probably start searching for other authors, writers, and industry experts. Search within bios for the particular terms you are interested in. You should also use hashtags to find people who are having conversations about your particular subject or industry. For instance, if you've written a book on tips and tricks for using the iPhone, then you might do a hashtag search (e.g., "#iPhone") to locate tweets and find people who are asking questions or looking for information about that item. You can then use the @Mention to answer these questions and make connections that way. Think of creative ways to use Twitter to make connections on the network that will be most advantageous to you.

In addition to suggestions offered under the "Who To Follow" button presented at the top of your home page, the following directories and software will make it a little easier to find followers and allow you to search by either topic, keyword, category, or location. When you have found some tweeps to follow, check who they're following to see if there's anyone who might be of interest to you.

Advanced Twitter Search (search.twitter.com)
You can find tweets based on words, people, places, dates, and attitudes (whether positive, negative, or inquisitive). For instance, "iPad :)" would find tweets with the word "iPad" that have a positive attitude associated with the product; "iPad :(" would find tweets with a negative attitude; and "iPad?" would find tweets that have questions about the iPad.

Just Tweet It (www.justtweetit.com)
A directory where you can find Tweeters with similar interests

Listorious (www.listorius.com)
Twitter people search and lists directory

Tweepz (www.tweepz.com)
This powerful engine lets you search for words within the bio, name, and location of other Twitter users. It also has certain functions where you can search for words starting with a certain letter or letters, search for adjacent words, as well as eliminate forbidden terms.

Tweet Adder (www.tweetadder.com)
This is a tool for serious Twitter users only. Available on Windows and Mac, Tweet Adder gives you the ability to put your Twitter search and follow activities on steroids. It features fully automated tweet posting and direct messaging, and its powerful search capabilities allow you to search and target people to follow based on the following:

- Tweet content and tweet location
- Profile information
- User location
- Followers of a particular user
- Users followed by a particular user
- All users within a specified user's list

Twellow (www.twellow.com)
Officially known as the Twitter yellow pages, Twello currently contains 30.5 million profiles and allows you to search by category.

Twellohood (www.twellow.com/twellowhood)
Twellohood is an extension of Twellow that allows you to search by location only.

Twibs (www.twibs.com)
A Twitter business directory

WeFollow (www.wefollow.com)
Use this tool to search by category (tag) and city.

Tip: Get listed by adding yourself to all the directories provided above.

When adding users, many will automatically follow you back, while others will require verification (more than likely through TrueTwit's validation service at www.truetwit.com) to ensure you're not a spammer. Whether or not to follow back everyone who follows you as a common courtesy has always been the subject of debate. Opinions are split pretty evenly on the subject, so you will have to make that determination yourself. You can choose to go with social etiquette, or you can choose to stick with your personal motives and ultimate reasons for being on Twitter. The latter allows you to have relevant, targeted users and content streams within your timeline. With the former, just about anything goes. The choice is yours.

Tip: Twitter provides you with the ability to block users. This prevents them from following you, sending you @Mentions, and adding you to their lists. To block a user, go to that user's page and click the gear icon, where you will be presented with the option to block. To unblock a user, just click on "Undo" from the blocked user's profile page.

If you eventually find the number of people you follow getting out of control, Twitter has a lists feature that allows you to organize people (both people you follow and people you don't) into groups or categories you define so that you can view just the tweet streams from particular groups. You may want to set up groups for authors, writers, journalists, and reviewers, etc. To add a user to a list, select the list icon on the user's page and check the box of the list you wish to add him or her to. To view your lists, click on the "Lists" tab presented on your home page. To see how many lists you have been added to, check the number that appears above "Listed" on your profile page. If you would like to automatically receive a direct message as soon as someone adds, removes, or changes you on any of their lists, follow @ListWatcher.

Figure 4: Twitter's List and Gear Icons

Well, you're pretty much good to go–and just in case you didn't catch it earlier, you can follow me on Twitter @lorraine_phill. I'll see you there!

Chapter 6:
Facebook Pages

Facebook. It's the social networking site that has over 500 million active users, 200 million of which access the site through mobile devices. There are 250 million log-ins per day, with an average of fifty-five minutes per visit. According to the Nielsen Company, global web users spend roughly five and a half hours per month on social networking sites, with Facebook accounting for the majority of the time reported.

Just in case you haven't heard, Facebook is the second most visited site on the Net, runner-up to none other than Google, and with statistics like that, Facebook should be an extremely important part of your Internet branding and marketing campaign. As an unparalleled distribution channel, with over 5 billion pieces of content (in the form of web links, news stories, blog posts, pictures, etc.) shared every day, Facebook offers you one of the most powerful tools to further establish your book and your brand's presence online.

Facebook Pages can be used to promote businesses, organizations, brands, products, artists, bands, public figures, entertainment products, or social causes. There's even an "Author" option that's available just for us. Pages are public (viewable to all whether registered on Facebook or not), and anyone can become a "fan" by simply "liking" your page. The top reasons for creating a Facebook Page include the following:

- Pages let you brand your own name with a Facebook URL that reads www.facebook.com/yournamehere. The only requirement is that you have more than twenty-five fans. You can register your personalized Facebook URL at www.facebook.com/username.
- Pages are crawled and indexed by search engines.
- Pages can have an unlimited number of fans.
- Pages are designed for business use, which makes it perfectly acceptable for you to use your page for promotional purposes.
- You can post to other Facebook Pages (but not to personal profiles) as your Page, which will result in increased exposure for your Page.
- You can create multiple Pages in case you need to promote more than one book or product.
- A Page can have more than one administrator assigned to it.
- Pages are fully customizable through the use of plug-ins or apps that allow you to incorporate additional links into your navigation system as needed to effectively communicate your brand.
- Each navigation link has its own dedicated URL, so you can select whichever one you'd like use as a landing page for visitors.
- You receive an email notification every time a user posts or comments on your Page. (This option can be switched off if preferred.)
- You receive weekly Facebook Page updates that provide statistics on the performance of your Page by email.
- You get access to Facebook Events, which is a FREE plug-in that allows you to plan, publicize, and promote events. You can invite guests; request RSVPs; manage your guest list; post discussions to the wall; and share links, photos, and videos pertinent to the event.
- Pages allow you to segment your professional writing life from your personal life, so ensure that your posts do the same.

Note: In case you're wondering, Facebook Groups have fewer features than Facebook Pages. Groups are better suited for businesses and brands that wish to build communities that connect people within a certain industry for discussion and informational purposes. Facebook Groups can be either public or private.

Steps to Setting Up Your Page

You can create and maintain a Facebook Page from your personal account. If you don't have a personal account yet, then set one up first. Here are the steps for creating a Facebook Page:

1. Log in to your Facebook account and click the "Advertising" link that appears at the bottom of the page. Don't worry, Pages are FREE.
2. Click on the "Facebook Page" link that appears within the text on the "Overview" tab.

Figure 5: Facebook Page Link

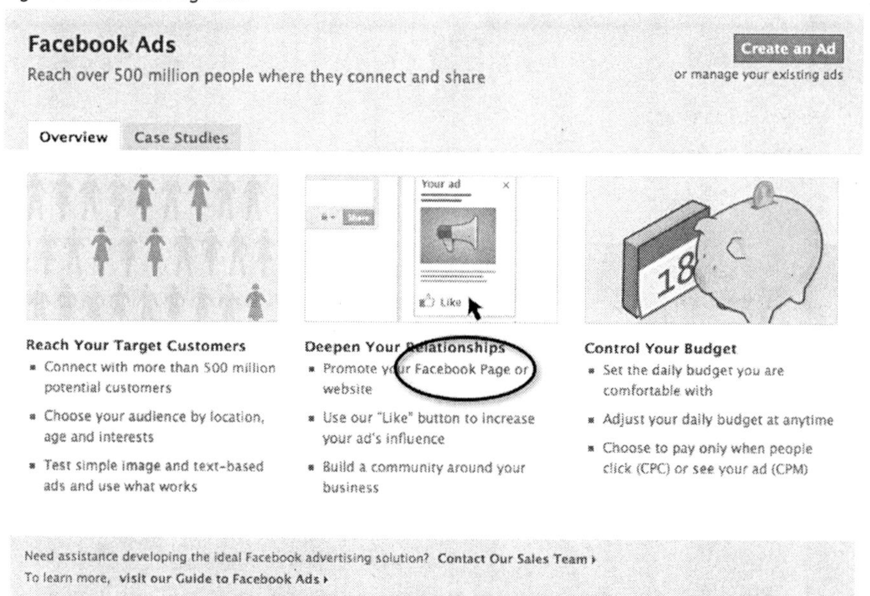

3. Hit the green "Create a Page" button that appears at the top left of the page.
4. From "Create a Page," depending on your requirements, select either "Author" from the "Artist, Band, or Public Figure" category or "Book" from the "Entertainment" category.

Figure 6: Facebook Page Categories

5. If you chose "Author," then simply fill in your name. You can use your real name, pen name, or a name that's in line with your brand. If, on the other hand, you selected "Book," then enter your book's title. For this option, I could choose to enter "Online Book Marketing" or "Online Book Marketing by Lorraine Phillips." Although this would result in a rather long URL, I can always shorten the URL later, when I have twenty-five fans.

   Tip: You may also choose to purchase a domain name and use it as a dedicated URL that forwards directly to your Facebook Page. The URL that leads directly to my Facebook Page is www.obm-fb.com. And yes, you can go ahead and "like" my Page!

6. Check the "I agree to Facebook Pages terms" box.
7. Click "Get Started" to complete creating your Page.

Things You Should Do

Facebook keeps a relatively uniform look and feel throughout the site, which means that the Facebook branded header and footer will remain the same regardless of what Page you are visiting or the features that are incorporated. As far as interfaces go, this is actually a good thing because uniformity creates familiarity, which means that users don't have to relearn the navigation system every time they visit a Page. To personalize your Page, you should do the following:

Upload an image. Your graphic can be up to 200 pixels wide and 600 pixels long, with a maximum file size of 4 megabytes. That's a decent amount of real estate to customize your page. Upload either your profile picture or your book's cover. You can have up to 600 pixels in length, so why don't you have the best of both worlds and create a graphic where your profile picture appears on top and your book cover image below?

Click on the "Info" link and "Edit Page" box to fill out the relevant information for your Page. This is your official introduction to the users who visit your Page. Tell them about yourself, your book, and what they can expect from your Page. Provide links to where your book can be purchased, whether on Amazon, your website, or other locations. List other ways they can connect with you, whether through your website, blog, Twitter, or LinkedIn. Describe what your book is about. Tell them why you wrote it, who it's for, and what benefits it provides. Because your Page will be crawled by search engines, make this information keyword rich. Include any interesting facts about yourself that users might not otherwise know. Of all the social networks, I find Facebook to be the most relaxed, mostly due to the informal "friends" aspect of the network and the way messages can quickly go viral between them. You may want to capitalize on the personal nature of the environment by showcasing pictures and videos, of both family and professional events. You set your own limits, but let visitors get the feeling that you are human, touchable, and reachable, just like them. And in reality, you are; this is ultimately what they will "buy" into and connect with. Engage users by regularly posting interesting and relevant content to your wall, where they can provide their feedback and comments. Make sure you show your presence by participating in conversations on a regular basis. Deepen your relationships and nurture your community by showing that you care. Start discussions on relevant topics, post interesting links, and alert users of any events you may be participating in or attending so that they can either attend or spread the word.

Tip: To set the landing page for your Facebook Page:
1. Click the "Wall" navigation link
2. Click the "Edit Page" button on the right
3. Select "Manage Permissions" from the left pane
4. Use the drop-down menu under the "Default Landing" tab to select your desired landing page

Customizing Your Page

You can further expand the functionality of your Facebook Page through the addition of apps, which appear as additional links on your Page (access through Edit Page > Apps). Make your page fun and engaging. Add in polls, share your blog content, incorporate a newsletter sign-up form, offer FREE ebook downloads, or integrate your Twitter and YouTube activities. For Facebook's application directory, you can visit www.facebook.com/apps/directory.php. Facebook does not list all the applications available for Pages, as quite a few of them are offered by third-party developers. You may have to do an Internet search to find developers for some of the specific applications or functionality you require.

You used to be able to create custom apps using FBML (which was Facebook's own version of HTML), but Facebook moved away from using FBML and now supports iFrame apps, which allow you to embed normal web pages that use HTML and CSS into the layout of a Page. Just so you know, Facebook announced that its decision to move away from FBML will not immediately affect any of the applications that currently exist or are in use; however, Facebook strongly recommends that you update those Pages to iFrame applications.

Having a customized app developed for your Page can be quite expensive, but you may decide to go this route instead of developing a full-blown website. Talk about pushing up the value of your brand, now you'll be joining the ranks of stars like Alicia Keys, and people might "like" your Page just for its apparent coolness, which can aid tremendously with your message going viral on the network. All in all, the more engaging features, functionality, and information you provide, the better.

Note: Remove links from your navigation menu that you are not using. To remove a link, click on the "Edit Page" button and select "Apps" from the left pane menu. You will be presented with a list of applications. Simply click on the "x" symbol next to a particular app and confirm to remove it.

Tools You Might Need

Facebook Apps from Involver (www.involver.com)

Involver is the Web's most trusted social marketing platform, providing applications and monitoring tools to over one hundred thousand brands and agencies. Here is a list of the FREE apps Involver provides.

File Sharing

Promote your exclusive media directly to Facebook, including video downloads, MP3s, ringtones, and more.

Flickr

Stream your photos to your Page in a format that adapts to updates and allows you to distribute your entire Flickr stream.

PDFs

Transform stand-alone documents like PDFs into Facebook-hosted web pages and share information instantaneously with your online audience, including white papers, menus, presentations, and other important materials.

Photo Gallery
Showcase your Flickr photos in a stunning and elegant carousel format.

RSS Feed
Syndicate your blog to the "News" link of your Facebook Page.

Slides
Display your catalogs, sales presentations, lesson plans, and big ideas on Facebook in a PowerPoint Deck format.

Twitter
Syndicate your Twitter feed directly to Facebook.

YouTube Channel
Deliver video directly to your social networks by incorporating your YouTube channel as a link on your Facebook Page.

More Facebook Customization Apps and Services (Paid and FREE)

HyperArts (www.hyperarts.com)
North Social (www.northsocial.com)
PageLever (www.pagelever.com)
Pagemodo (www.pagemodo.com)
ShopTab (www.shoptab.net)
SplashTab (www.splashtab.com)
Static 520 (www.static520.com)
Tabfusion (www.tabfusion.com)
TabSite (www.facebooktabsite.com)
Wildfire Promotion Builder (wildfireapp.com)

Simultaneously Update Facebook, Twitter, and Other Social Networking Sites

HootSuite (www.hootsuite.com)
Ping.fm (ping.fm)
SocialOomph (www.socialoomph.com)

Apps for Your Phone or Mobile Device

Blackberry – Facebook (www.blackberry.com/smartphones/features/social/facebook.jsp)
iPhone, iPad, and iPod Touch – Facebook (www.facebook.com/iphone)
iPhone, iPad, iPod Touch, and Android – Hellotxt (hellotxt.com)
Windows Mobile – Facebook (comes preinstalled)

Other

Facebook Badges (www.facebook.com/badges)
Facebook Social Plug-ins (developers.facebook.com/plugins)

Tip: Keep up-to-date on all Facebook developments by visiting http://blog.facebook.com.

Promoting Your Page

For people to "like" your Page, they have to find out about it. The more "likes" you have, the more credibility, so get to work publicizing your Page. Here are some ideas:

- Invite Facebook friends who may be interested in your subject matter.
- Strategically post to other relevant Facebook Pages to increase exposure of your Page.
- Join Facebook Groups within your industry, meet others who share your interests, and let them know about your Page.
- Send emails to family, friends, and associates announcing your Page.

- Use other social media networks (such as Twitter, LinkedIn, and YouTube) to publicize your Page.
- Write an article for your blog or newsletter inviting people to join your Page.
- Add a "Like" button to your website or blog. When a user clicks on the button, a story appears in his or her friends' News Feed that includes a link back to your site.
- Add a "Like" box to your website or blog, which enables users to both like your Facebook Page as well as view its stream directly from your site.
- Add a "Page Badge" to your site or blog to share your Facebook Page information on your site; a badge displays your picture, name, and a brief description of your Page.
- Encourage fans to add a "Like" badge to their blog or website, which shows that a user has liked a Page.
- Include a button or link to your Page as part of your email signature, so it is seen by all with whom you correspond.
- Add your Facebook Page URL to business cards, flyers, bookmarks, and any other promotional materials you have.
- Create book buzz by holding a contest and offering a great giveaway.
- Share your Page link on message boards and forums; offer good, reputable information; and make your Facebook URL a part of your signature there also.

So now that we're finished with Facebook, temporarily of course, let's head over to LinkedIn!

Chapter 7:
LinkedIn

LinkedIn is a professional social networking site with over 100 million members worldwide. Touting a good mix of savvy networkers and executives from a wide range of industries, LinkedIn reports user demographics of 52 percent male and 48 percent female. What's more, 68 percent of LinkedIn users are over the age of 35; compared to the slightly younger demographic that can be found on both Facebook and Twitter. Not surprisingly, LinkedIn attracts a well-educated, affluent audience, with 69 percent of members earning annual salaries in excess of $60,000 and a staggering 75 percent of members possessing a college degree or higher. The real power of LinkedIn lies in your ability to grow your network exponentially, giving you access to potential readers, industry professionals, resources, opportunities, and subject matter experts with whom you can exchange knowledge, information, and ideas.

Your first-degree network consists of the people you know and have directly connected with, while your second-degree network consists of the people your connections know. Those linked to your second-degree network then make up your third-degree network. In this way, you are not only linked to past and present friends, classmates, peers, clients, colleagues, and associates, but you are also indirectly linked to everyone they know as well, providing you a basis on which to meet others and widen your network as far as you see fit.

> **Note:** People beyond your third-degree network appear as "out of your network." If you would like to connect with users deemed "out of your network," then simply become a member of a Group they belong to and send an invitation request that way. As long as they haven't changed the default Group settings that allow members within a Group to contact one another, then your request will be received.

To add someone to your network, that person has to actually accept your invitation, whether it came directly from you (where you indicated the recipient as a colleague, classmate, or friend) or there was somewhat of a formal introduction from one of your connections. When on the receiving end of an invitation and you decide to connect with a fellow user, always reply with a message thanking him or her for the opportunity to connect, including a brief summary of what you do, why you might be of benefit to that user's network, and other ways he or she can connect with you.

Setting Up Your Profile

To get established on LinkedIn, it's going to be necessary for you to fill out your profile information in a way that will ultimately make people want to engage and connect. Your profile should summarize your professional expertise, experience, and accomplishments. Use powerful, searchable words (or keywords) to describe your skills, talents, and specialties. Because LinkedIn currently receives about one sign-up per second, the site ranks highly in Google. Thought and consideration should be taken when creating your profile so that you might take advantage of the SEO techniques described in previous chapters. Think of the specific keywords that a recruiter might use when searching for a job candidate within your industry. Are these words within your profile?

Most people develop their profile as an extension of their resume, but what they fail to do is include the benefits or services they provide that can be of value to a prospective connection. Make sure your profile not only describes who you are and what you do, but also lets people know how you and your skills can possibly be of value to them. We are back to that old question: "What's in it for me?" How can you be of use? Why should someone want to connect with you? Why would someone purchase a copy of your book or maybe even hire you to speak, teach, write, or lecture? Your profile should explicitly answer these questions.

Upload your super friendly, inviting, professional picture. Don't post the holiday picture with you in your sombrero in Mexico; this is just not the network for that. As previously indicated, try to keep your picture consistent across all social networks so that you are easily recognizable. Pay special attention to your headline, as it will be the first thing people read on your profile. This headline also appears alongside any posts you make on the site. Make sure that your headline is fairly descriptive and contains at least one major keyword that may be searched on within your industry (e.g., author, writer, AJAX programmer, or business consultant).

> **Note:** Although filling out your LinkedIn profile may seem like a long and tedious process compared to the other social networks, according to LinkedIn, users with fully complete profiles are forty times more likely to find opportunities through the site than those who have incomplete or partial profiles.

Do not use the default URL that is initially assigned to your account. Edit the link found under Public Profile to customize your URL to include your first and last name. If that's not available, find something as close as possible, maybe incorporating your middle initial. My LinkedIn URL is www.linkedin.com/in/lorrainephillips. Use your URL in forum and email signatures, in author resource boxes (as described in the next chapter), and anywhere else you can think of on the Web in order to create backlinks to your profile that help boost your page rankings.

You also have the ability to link to three external websites, such as your personal website, company website, blog, RSS feed, or portfolio, from within your profile (see Figure 7 overleaf). Use descriptive terms for these links. For instance, instead of using the default "Company Website," I could select "Other" from the drop-down menu that is presented and

Figure 7: Example of Linking External Websites

Additional Information

Websites:	Other:	Online Book Marketing	http://www.onlinebookbı	Clear
	Other:	Lorraine Phillips	http://www.lorraine-philli	Clear
	Other:	360 Books	http://www.3sixtybooks.	Clear

enter the term "360 Books" as the text that will show up for my business's hyperlink. As you fill out your profile, aim to use best SEO practices. Make sure to keep your profile both current and somewhat consistent across all social networks.

> **Tip:** Use one of your external links to directly link to your book title as featured on your website or blog. Better yet, link directly to its listing on Amazon.

PROFILE EXTRAS

After your profile is complete, consider adding these applications (as found under Edit Profile; scroll down to Applications > Add an Application) to enhance your listing.

Add Your Publication Information

LinkedIn gets better and better. The network recently added a section where you can include patents and publications. Need I say more? Add in your title, the name of your publisher, publication date, website URL, and your book's summary, and you are good to go!

Link to Your Blog

Blog Link is an application that lets you connect your blog directly to your professional profile, giving you the opportunity to get in front of this audience in a way that allows you to connect people to your blog, drive traffic to your site, further expose your brand, and showcase your knowledge and expertise. Blog headlines along with a few introductory sentences are displayed on your profile, and all visitors have to do is click the headline, and they'll immediately be transported over to your site where the post can be viewed in full. Hopefully you have some type of free offer available to capture the email addresses of these random visitors so that you can build ongoing relationships with them. Blog Link supports various platforms such as TypePad, Movable Type, Vox, WordPress.com, WordPress.org, Blogger, and LiveJournal.

> **Note:** There is also a WordPress utility available that allows you to sync your WordPress blog posts with your LinkedIn profile and offers the ability to filter your posts through the use of a special LinkedIn tag.

Add Your Book Title to Amazon's Reading List Application

This application was developed for people within certain industries to be able to share and rate the books they are reading or list books they are planning to read. Capitalize on the functionality of this app by adding and exposing your own book title. Don't you just love being an author?

Add a SlideShare Presentation

SlideShare allows you to display presentations and documents on your LinkedIn profile, accepting PPT, PPS, PPTX, PDF, DOC, DOCX, Keynote, and iWork file formats. You can upload portfolios, resumes, PDFs, marketing and sales presentations, or whatever you may need. You also have the ability to embed YouTube videos into your page. I have used this functionality to display book trailers on my profile page. SlideShare can even sync with Facebook, allowing you to upload to any one of the networks (SlideShare, Facebook, or LinkedIn) and instantly displaying the item in question on all three.

Use the Events Application

Similar to the offering on Facebook, LinkedIn's events application allows you to see what events members of your entire professional network are attending as well as find events that are recommended for you based on your industry and job function. What a great way to meet potential book purchasers and make professional contacts in person! Now you know about tradeshows, conferences, and training events where they may be converging. You'll be able to see who's attending and who's interested. You can also put important conferences on your profile and show when you are presenting or exhibiting.

Use the LinkedIn Polls Application

The LinkedIn Polls application allows you to poll your network for answers to any query you may have and can aid in gathering market research data.

Things You Should Know and Do

Know What's Public and Private on LinkedIn

Users within your first-, second-, and third-degree networks can see your full profile listing, while those outside your network only get to see a limited view of the information. Only users in your first-degree network actually see your email address listed on your profile page. Non-LinkedIn users get to see your Public Profile, which by default includes your name, title, location, industry, number of connections, and number of recommendations. To change these default settings, find your name that appears as a text link at the very top right of the screen. Click the arrow that appears next to your name to reveal the Settings option. Click Settings > Profile Settings: Public Profile and make the necessary changes.

Join Groups

As of this writing, there are more than 730,000 different groups on LinkedIn, which can be accessed from the main menu under Groups > Groups Directory. Becoming a member of, and actively participating in, groups that are relevant to your industry is another way to increase your profile's visibility and make industry contacts. Much like the forums found on the Internet, LinkedIn groups center around common interests, themes, topics, or industries. Here you can discuss issues, job opportunities, solve problems, gain new insights, discover industry trends, and–most importantly–establish your expert status within your industry. You have to actually join a group before you can view the discussions taking place, so upon requesting to join a group, you will either be accepted right away and be allowed to proceed into the forum or your status will be changed to pending, where it will be manually reviewed and hopefully approved by a group owner. You will receive your approval notification by email. Check the box that allows you to receive a daily or weekly digest from the group (sent over email), so you can see whether there are any relevant discussions going on that you want to participate in. Get to know the knowledge leaders within your industry, and if you feel they can be of benefit to your network (and vice versa), then send them official invitations to connect.

Start a Group

Starting a group on LinkedIn (Groups > Create a Group) is a great way to position yourself as a leader within your particular industry, giving you the ability to connect like-minded individuals for the purpose of information exchange. You should take time to build your own network first so that you already have associations in place with people who might be interested in joining your group and participating in your group's discussions. Research similar groups to see if their communities are active and flourishing or if there are any gaps you could possibly fill. As with any online community, it will take passion and commitment to grow your group. You will need to promote its existence through various channels as well as regularly post topics of interest that encourage conversation between members. As group owner, you can assign roles such as "group manager" or "group moderator" to other members of the site so that they can assist you with group management and maintenance. You also have the ability to email group members and send out weekly digests of group activity. Find creative ways to use your LinkedIn group to drive targeted traffic to your website or blog.

Become an Expert with LinkedIn Answers

LinkedIn Answers (accessed from More > Answers) provides a means for you to ask and answer industry-related questions. On entering the section, you will be presented with two panes that appear within a speech bubble at the top of the screen. The left pane allows you to enter a question (which you will need to categorize after completion), and the right pane gives a list of the recommended categories in which you can provide answers. Underneath the speech bubble, you will see a list of "New Questions From Your Network" and "This Week's Top Experts." That's where you eventually want to be listed. Hunt down the questions within your category of expertise that are related to your book's topic, and if you can add something of value, then go ahead and contribute. After a question has been open for seven days, it is usually closed, and the individual who submitted the question is asked to select the best answer. Every time your entry is selected as the best answer, you gain an expertise point that lets you appear on the "Top Experts" list. The more expertise points you earn, the higher you appear on the list. This expert status is also added to your profile. By continually providing great answers, you will become known over time as an expert within your field, giving you a wonderful opportunity to increase visibility and build brand equity.

Get Recommendations

One way of making your profile stand out and increasing your credibility is by getting recommendations from those in your immediate network. It looks great when someone you've worked with takes the time to give you a personal recommendation. Find people who you've worked with and either ask them for a recommendation or provide a recommendation for them in the hopes that they might return the favor. These comments give you the opportunity to highlight characteristics about yourself that you may have overlooked or taken for granted and as a result failed to include in your profile. You are unable to modify the recommendations you receive, which increases the believability and validity of these comments. Use the LinkedIn recommendation tool (Profile > Recommendations) to send a personalized request that politely asks for a recommendation. Let the recipient know your objective for receiving a recommendation, provide a couple sentences to help him or her get started, and describe what types of comments you are looking for. Don't forget to thank those who oblige.

Note: You need at least three recommendations before LinkedIn will mark your profile as being 100 percent complete.

Get Listed in LinkedIn's Service Provider Directory

LinkedIn has a Service Provider Directory that is comparable to a Yellow Pages of credible professional services as recommended by members of the network. You are unable to add yourself to the directory. For you to be added to the directory, LinkedIn requires that a client give you a recommendation, selecting the "Service Provider" option. (Other options include Colleague, Business Partner, and Student.) Upon being recommended as a Service Provider, your profile information will be listed under the relevant category. To access or view the directory, click on "Companies," where you'll see the "Service Provider" text link across to the right.

Note: It is not necessary to have a LinkedIn account to be listed in the directory. For a member to make a recommendation, all that is needed is the service provider's name and email address.

Create a Company Profile

If you own a business or are a solopreneur, then you may want to take advantage of LinkedIn's Create a Company Profile feature. It can be accessed through Companies and then the "Add a Company" text link or button (see Figure 8 overleaf) that appears on the right. Only current employees can register a company, and the only requirement is that you have a unique company-owned email domain (so no Yahoo!, Gmail, or Hotmail extensions). It will be necessary for you to confirm your email address before being allowed to proceed with the registration, where you can then add admins; upload your logo; give a company description,

Figure 8: Create a Company Profile

including specialties; and provide a link to the company's Twitter ID or blog's RSS feed. You can also choose whether to have your company featured in the LinkedIn news module that appears on your home page to update colleagues on all your company's developing news. Much like individuals, companies can also receive recommendations. LinkedIn users have the ability to access your company profile when viewing your personal profile.

Update Your Status

Similar to Facebook and Twitter, LinkedIn allows you to provide status updates by simply accessing the status box on your home page. Update your network regarding any progress you make with your book or other projects. You can elect to make each individual post visible to those in your network only (who can then add comments) or to anyone who accesses your LinkedIn profile. There is a 700-character limit, but if you check the Twitter box, then that limit is truncated down to 140 characters. It is also possible to connect your Twitter account to LinkedIn, so you can make status updates directly from your Twitter account. It will be necessary to add "#in" or "#li" to your tweets for the posts to show on LinkedIn. LinkedIn cleverly filters @Mentions so that they don't show up in your profile along with your other posts.

Remove a Contact

For whatever reason, if you decide that you would like to remove a connection from your network, click on "Contacts," then click the "Remove

Connections" link that appears on the upper right. Select the person(s) you would like to remove and click on the "Remove Connections" button. When you remove a contact, he or she is not notified of your actions, but your information "magically" disappears from his or her contacts list.

Go Mobile

LinkedIn gives you the power to stay connected on the go, and there are FREE apps available for iPhone, Blackberry, and Palm. Visit the LinkedIn site for more details. For all other phones access http://m.linkedin.com from your mobile device.

Building Your Network

To initially build your network, go to Contacts > Add Connections, where you can import your web email contacts from Hotmail, Gmail, MSN, Yahoo!, and various other services. You can also import your contacts from your desktop email clients, such as Outlook and Apple Mail, in the CSV, TXT, or VCF formats. You can invite colleagues (according to the companies listed in your profile) or classmates (according to your listed education), and LinkedIn has a tab that provides a list of "People You May Know," which uses its proprietary "secret sauce" algorithm to help you find other users with common interests who you may be interested in linking with.

Next, invite people in your address book who you feel could benefit from LinkedIn but may not be a part of the network already. Send them a customized email explaining why you think they should join and how the network may be beneficial to them. After you have your first-degree network in place, then it's time to start reaching out to the people they know, who are currently in your second-degree network. Match your network to your industry, identifying people who you think can help you achieve your goals or to whom you can provide some type of value or service. Request introductions, clearly stating how you could be of benefit to one another or revealing what interests and goals you have in common. Give them a reason to want to become a part of your network. You can also use the Advanced People Search (top right on the toolbar) to find people according to:

- Keywords
- First Name
- Last Name
- Title
- Company
- School
- Location
- Country
- Postal Code
- A certain distance or mile radius
- Industry (currently listing 147 different industries as well as the option to select "All")
- Relationship (defined as all LinkedIn members, first-degree connections, second-degree connections, group members, or third-degree connections and everyone else)
- Language

Search results can be saved for later use and can be sorted by relevance, relationship, relationship and recommendations, connections, or keywords. Don't just hoard connections for yourself, however. Regularly make recommendations (and introductions) to others for connections and contacts that may be useful to their network. Lastly, networking is not just a numbers game; it's quality over quantity. Remember to not only build relationships, but maintain them by looking out for those in your network too. Regularly provide useful information and valuable ideas that can help your connections out in some way. And yes, of course, you are allowed to tap into that network for whatever it is you may need as well. It's the good old law of reciprocity!

Note: Smart Bees (www.smartbees.biz) offers a paid service that can extract the details of your second-degree contacts and provide a spreadsheet that contains the following information: name, title, location, industry, company, position, education, profile URL, number of connections, and the name of the first-degree contact that connects you. This is an extremely valuable tool for the LinkedIn power user.

Tip: To find out about the latest and greatest on LinkedIn, you can visit LinkedIn's official blog at blog.linkedin.com.

PART IV

Other Vehicles for Online Marketing

Chapter 8:
Article Marketing

The easiest way to sell a product or service is by giving some of it away for FREE. According to e-commerce consultant Dr. Ralph F. Wilson, *free* is the most powerful word in any marketer's vocabulary. The simple reason is because FREE attracts attention (at least legitimate offers do), and the new rule of the Web is first FREE, then sell.

Article marketing is the process of making your articles available for publishing to a wide range of article directories. As an author, you can use article marketing to give content and information away in the hopes of attracting attention not only to the book (or upcoming book) you have for sale, but to any other product or service you may offer as well. Article marketing is an extremely powerful tool and one of the most effective means of online marketing, allowing you to:

- Get FREE publicity for your book
- Increase your brand's visibility
- Gain credibility and further establish yourself as an authority or expert in your field
- Showcase your credentials and bio information
- Help your target audience find you
- Drive targeted traffic to your website or blog

- Increase book sales
- Increase newsletter subscriptions
- Reach a wider audience by featuring content on respected, established sites that already have high rankings in Google
- Automatically notify your RSS feed subscribers of new articles you have published
- Generate quality backlinks that help increase your site's search engine rankings
- Increase exposure through viral marketing (better known as word-of-mouth or word-of-mouse marketing), as other publishers–who already have their own audiences–reprint your content in exchange for attribution and links
- Generate media interest

When constructing your article, always keep your brand and what you'd like to be known for at the forefront of your mind. A powerful brand should be somewhat consistent over various mediums. You can't be a complete jokester on Twitter and a serious, intellectual boffin elsewhere, as you just won't be believable. Although it's okay to mix it up a little, try not to deviate too far from the norm, wherever that is for you.

Address your target audience with benefit-oriented headlines that appeal directly to their wants and needs. Make sure to employ the SEO techniques discussed in previous chapters. Start by crafting your keyword-rich title, placing special attention on the first four words. Although your title must be descriptive, it should be concise–the fewer words you have in your title, the more importance Google gives to each word. After your title is created, use it to direct content creation.

It goes without saying that your articles should be 100 percent original and feature content that has a centralized topic or theme in line with your book's subject matter. Submitted articles should be between 400 and 800 words long. Personally, I aim for my articles to be no longer than 600 words, as it's been proven that shorter articles achieve a higher distribution rate than longer ones. Think quality, not quantity!

> **Note:** Do not submit the exact same material that appears on your website or blog without significantly updating and rewriting the content first. Keep your website and blog content unique.

Never blatantly make a sales pitch in your article. Although you are looking for increased exposure and sales, your first objective is to provide valuable information that either solves a problem, satisfies a need, or answers a question. You get the chance to show off your credentials at the end of the article in what is known as a "resource box." Your resource box should be short and to the point. It should include the following:

- Your name
- Your credentials (e.g., a PhD, certification, award, or some type of industry recognition)
- A brief bio
- Publication information of the book(s) you have published that are related to the category of the article you are submitting
- Your website's URL
- Direct contact information
- A call to action

The whole idea behind article writing is to generate interest, traffic, brand equity, and sales, so your call to action should get readers to act in some way, shape, or form. The content of your article is what attracted readers in the first place, so your resource box should play on their interest in a way that encourages them to click through to your site. Drive traffic to your site by offering a free sample chapter, monthly newsletter, report, podcast, or ebook, making sure to capture the email addresses of these targeted visitors when they arrive. Always include a plain text version of the link to your site within your resource box just in case any other links you have provided get lost in translation. Check some of the authors on the directories listed in the next section for ideas on what your resource box should say.

FREE Article Marketing Directories

All directories have unique submission guidelines, so it will be necessary for you to check with each one to ensure you are complying with its particular set of rules. Know that most (although not all) will manually verify your content before approving your article for publication on their websites. As of this writing, the top ten article directories, filtered by both traffic and Google PageRank, are as follows:

1. EzineArticles.com (www.ezinearticles.com)
2. HubPages (www.hubpages.com)
3. Articlesbase (www.articlesbase.com)
4. Buzzle.com (www.buzzle.com)
5. eHow (www.ehow.com)
6. Suite101 (www.suite101.com)
7. Helium (www.helium.com)
8. GoArticles (www.goarticles.com)
9. ArticleSnatch (www.articlesnatch.com)
10. Article Alley (www.articlealley.com)

Tip: For a list of the top fifty article directories by traffic and PageRank, visit www.vretoolbar.com/articles/directories.php.

It is estimated that 80 percent of article directories do not accept submissions that have links within the body of an article. If you submit to a directory where links are accepted, then use your keyword phrases to link to the pages of your site (or others) that match or correspond to that particular phrase. Because of the way Google's algorithm works, ensure that all keyword phrases within an article link to DIFFERENT URLs. All your keyword phrases should not just link to your home page; instead, your keyword phrases should link to different pages within your site (or other sites online). The links you provide should be used to further enhance the reader's experience and not as just another SEO technique to get visitors over to your site. If that is the case, and your links are not appropriate, then you risk your article being rejected by the directory. Most directories allow you to submit a list of the keywords that should accompany your article. Use the keyword list you created earlier and select wisely.

You can submit the same article to each and every directory listed, but check the guidelines, as some do require exclusivity. There is a myth that submitting an article to numerous directories creates duplicate content, which results in your article being penalized or discounted in search engine results. Lucky for us, this myth is not true. Article syndication is no different from news syndication, where the exact same news story is blasted over the Web thousands of times without any penalty whatsoever. When you hold the exclusive copyright to an article, you may do with it what you please.

Note: Most article directories allow you to instantly share the fact that you just published an article to Facebook, Twitter, and other social networking sites with the click of a button.

To be successful as an article marketer, you will need to invest considerable time to the distribution of your articles online. The process of submitting your articles to directories is long, tedious, and boring to say the least. No fireworks here, but the payoff over time is well worth the effort. There are article submission services that claim to automatically submit your articles to numerous directories at a time, but because of the different requirements of each directory, I would steer clear of these types of services and instead hire help to manually perform the task. It may take several months before you start seeing any results from your marketing efforts, but eventually you should see an increase in the traffic to your site as well as higher Google rankings in searches performed for your selected keywords, which should translate into an increase in book sales or, at the very least, newsletter subscriptions.

To solidify yourself as an expert in your field, it is imperative that you build, build, build your brand by consistently delivering high-quality content to these directories and producing at least one article every two weeks. Doing it this way will allow you to build awareness, credibility, and trust over time. Eventually you'll become the go-to person from whom people feel comfortable buying products and services because in their eyes, you've established a relationship with them by consistently providing FREE, valuable information that they need.

Chapter 9:
Email Marketing

I believe email marketing is the most personal form of online marketing there is, as email does not have the abandon rate of social networks such as MySpace, Facebook, and Twitter. Facebook and Twitter might be the hot things right now, but nobody can guarantee that they still will be in the future. Most people keep their email accounts forever; that's why building your email list should be your NUMBER ONE online marketing activity. I still check my personal Yahoo! account daily after twelve years of use, so it's very likely that you can continue to communicate with your subscribers for years to come. With this combination of virtual direct marketing and personal communication, you now have your target audience in the palm of your hand, giving you the ultimate opportunity to build strong, lasting relationships with them.

Email marketing is similar to article marketing except you're sending information directly to people who have decided to opt in, or subscribe, to your newsletter. Email marketing through opt in newsletters allows you to:

- Regularly communicate with your target audience
- Provide something of value to readers
- Increase site traffic
- Increase sales

- Nurture and build lasting, profitable relationships
- Build trust and credibility
- Establish yourself as an expert
- Encourage customer loyalty
- Keep your name in the front of customers' minds

To get visitors to subscribe to your newsletter, if your design allows, boldly place your newsletter sign-up form at the top left of every page of your site. Wherever you decide to place the form, keep design consistent by placing it in the exact same spot on every page, always presenting visitors with the option to sign up, no matter what page of your site they may land at. Increase trust and your user's willingness to divulge email information by including verbiage on the form similar to "This information will be used for correspondence only. We respect your privacy, and your email address will never be shared, sold, or rented." And of course, follow through with your promise. Display a page after a user subscribes that asks the subscriber to add your email address to his or her "whitelist" to avoid the possibility of your emails getting canned in the subscriber's spam folder.

> **Tip:** Most ISP's consider HTML-only emails as more likely to be spam than text-only emails. Get past these filters by using a combination of both HTML and text in your newsletter, which is known as a "multipart MIME" message.

When you begin sending out your newsletter, your email heading (or subject line) should be relevant and appropriate to your target market so that the recipient will not be tempted to hit delete before even opening it. Ensure that your benefit-oriented headline is clear and intriguing, containing enough information to persuade the reader to open your email and read on. Your heading should not exceed eighty characters. Because some email clients truncate subject lines that are longer than fifty characters, make sure that the words with the biggest impact are communicated near the beginning of your subject line. Otherwise, you risk your email being dismissed by the recipient if the subject line happens to get truncated.

Note: For a list of 100 subject line spam filter triggers that should never be used, see Appendix C on page 191.

Really use your content-rich newsletter to empathize with your audience's needs. Give them a reason to not only subscribe, but to stay subscribed. Entice them to subscribe with some type of FREE offer, such as a sample chapter, report, podcast, or ebook. Encourage them to stay by providing engaging content that includes surveys, polls, and links to discussion boards where they can give their feedback, comments, and suggestions. Get them involved in order to encourage click-throughs to your site where they can find additional information and updates.

Tip: Include back issues of your newsletter on your website or blog in both HTML and downloadable PDF formats.

Don't give your subscribers a reason to leave or unsubscribe by being irritating and obtrusive. I suggest emailing about once per month, possibly twice if you have that much great information to share. Ensure that you are actually sharing information and not just sending out a sales pitch. I think it's quite acceptable to end your email with your credentials and book information, much like the resource box used in article marketing. Provide links or icons that link to your Facebook, Twitter, or LinkedIn accounts to help boost your social media activities, too. Also, it is common courtesy (and the law within the United States) to allow readers a way to opt out of your newsletter should they no longer wish to receive it, so make sure to include an easy opt-out process in all the newsletters that you send.

It's a proven fact that people just don't buy the first time around. It can take between two to seven exposures (or emails) before they even consider getting their wallets out. Your main objective is to convert your readers into paying customers, purchasing your book or any other service you provide. The way to do that (much like article marketing) is to consistently provide content that's current, useful, valuable, answers questions, or offers solutions.

Managing Your Email List

There are top-notch email marketing services offered by companies such as AWeber (www.aweber.com), Constant Contact (www.constantcontact.com), iContact (www.icontact.com), and Mad Mimi (www.madmimi.com). Of these services, Mad Mimi is the most affordable. These services charge anywhere from $9.95 to $699 per month to automate and manage your email marketing campaign. Their features are extensive and impressive, but if you're not selling high-priced information products or consulting services in addition to your book(s), then I have another recommendation that will initially provide better value for your money.

I highly recommend the email marketing software GroupMail (www.group-mail.com). I have been successfully using this software for over ten years. And I unashamedly am probably still using the same version I purchased ten years ago, but that just shows how good it is.

GroupMail is available on the Windows platform, and the personal edition is priced at $160. It's one of those products that you just can't live without, and it will pay for itself time and time again. It is absolute child's play to use. You can easily import addresses and mail to lists of any size. The largest list I have mailed to consisted of about 22,000 subscribers; the software did not choke, cough, or even sputter. Incidentally, mailing to this many subscribers using one of the services mentioned earlier would have cost me $150 just for the month.

> **Tip:** Check with your host provider to find out the number of emails you are allowed to send out each day, as there are limits that may make it necessary for you to split your emailing activities over a few days.

GroupMail's list management and organization is a breeze, and it automates the processing of opt-in, opt-out, and bounced emails. When somebody opts in for your newsletter, he or she is automatically added to the your mailing list. When somebody opts out of your newsletter, he or she is automatically removed from your database list. If an email address is no longer active, which results in the email coming back (or being bounced), then this defunct address is also automatically removed from your list.

GroupMail sends autoresponses and can process "double opt-ins." A double opt-in means a visitor who subscribes to your newsletter receives an email asking him or her to confirm subscription by clicking on a link provided in the email. Only after clicking this link will the visitor's address be added to your database. Doing it this way cuts down on the chance of receiving fake email addresses from spambots or other means, as a real person has to confirm his or her subscription from a live, functioning email address. GroupMail comes with thirty-eight HTML email newsletter templates. There's a FREE version available online, but accessing the full features described above will require actually purchasing the personal edition.

Note: To receive a 25 percent discount from Infacta for GroupMail email marketing and newsletter software, send an email to sales@infacta.com with the subject line "Online Book Marketing Discount" or visit www.onlinebookbuzz.com to access the discount link.

Chapter 10:
Audio Podcasts

An audio podcast is a prerecorded audio file that can either be streamed online or made available for download and listened to on a personal computer or mobile device. Podcast use has exploded in recent years, and audio podcasts provide an efficient and effective way for you to build credibility, attract customers, generate traffic, and of course, create book buzz. The advantage of using podcasts is that it's currently a lot less competitive than the article marketing scene. Your podcast can be syndicated, subscribed to, and automatically downloaded (or "fed") to a subscriber's computer (or mobile device) via RSS every time new offerings become available.

Audio extends your reach in a different way from other mediums, as now your message can be delivered to your audience while they're on the move, whether driving to work, working out, taking a lunch break, or riding the bus. Your audience can listen to you just about anywhere they are able to carry a portable device. You can present specialized information, breaking news, or new developments related to your industry; give opinions; make observations; conduct interviews; or record your lectures, workshops, and seminars. Whatever you feel your audience will find useful and engaging is what you need to offer. Ask for input and feedback from your listeners to not only find out how you're doing, but also to poll for topics they would like to hear discussed in the future.

Creating Your Podcast

To create an audio podcast you will need the following:

A computer. Either a Mac or a PC will do the job.

A headset with microphone. I use the Plantronics Audio 470 USB folding headset and microphone that works with both Macs and PCs and produces excellent results.

Audio editing software. You can use GarageBand on the Mac and Audacity (audacity.sourceforge.net) on the PC. Audacity is available for FREE and is multiplatform, which means there is also a version available for the Mac.

Start your podcast with a brief introduction so that listeners will know what to expect during the show. Sound natural. Just be yourself. Don't try to put on your best "broadcaster" voice like the ones you've heard the professionals use on the radio, or you'll come off sounding fake and phony. Just speak as if you're talking with a bunch of friends. Record in a noise-free environment. Don't forget to turn off your cell phone, put the pets away, and check the air conditioner settings. Use fade-ins and fade-outs at the beginning and end of your show so that it sounds professional. Let the passion and know-how you have for your subject shine through. Don't ramble. Speak clearly and confidently, so it sounds like you really know what you're talking about. You may want to create a brief script prior to recording to help keep you on track.

Know that audio quality is relatively important. We are in the digital age, so folks no longer want to hear the familiar hiss of cassette tapes from back in the day. Neither do they want to hear extreme fluctuations in the volume of your voice, forcing them to continually adjust the volume control to compensate. Unless you have engineering experience, you're not going to produce pristine audio the first time around. It'll take trial and error for you to create something you can live with. But don't obsess about it either. With dedication, commitment, and possibly some help, you'll get the results you want over time. In order of importance, it's content and delivery first, then quality.

When recording, make sure your levels don't go into the red or over the 0-decibel mark on the meter. If that happens, your audio will be "clipped," and you'll end up with a distorted track. Just back off the mic a little or bring down the mic's volume to accommodate. If you make any mistakes or hiccups along the way, just keep recording (repeating the section again), as these parts can be edited out later on, and your listeners will never know the difference.

Note: For an excellent podcast creation guide, visit www.podcast411.com/podcast101. This tutorial covers creating and editing audio; encoding to MP3; adding ID3 tags; setting up RSS; and submitting podcasts to iTunes, Zune, and Blackberry.

Although the subject at hand should really dictate your podcast's length, ten to fifteen minutes of audio is a good place to start. You can choose to keep it simple, featuring your voice only, or you can add background music and sound effects to jazz things up a bit. Remember, it is illegal to use copyrighted music in your podcast without acquiring the proper licenses first.

Tip 1: For FREE royalty-free music loops and effects, visit these sites:
Flash Kit (www.flashkit.com/links/Sounds/Free_SFX/)
Freesound (www.freesound.org)
Partners In Rhyme (www.partnersinrhyme.com/pir/free_music_loops.shtml)

Tip 2: For pristine quality, royalty-free music files that start at $1, visit AudioJungle (www.audiojungle.net).

Make your podcast both user- and SEO-friendly by creating an accurate, descriptive summary of the contents of your show. This is your sales pitch to both potential listeners and search engines. Put relevant keywords in the title and throughout the body of your text, so if your subject is searched for online, you'll have an increased chance of your podcast showing up in results.

As with your other marketing efforts, you're not going to build a cult following overnight, but if you keep your podcasts consistently coming with great content, then just like cream, you'll eventually rise to the top. With that said, it's important to have a schedule (whether weekly, fortnightly, monthly, etc.) so that folks know exactly when to expect delivery of files. Adhering to a schedule shows your level of commitment and professionalism, and there's no harm done if you pop an unexpected podcast in every now and again, too, as that just shows dedication.

Tip: If you are interested in creating an online radio show, check out BlogTalkRadio (www.blogtalkradio.com).

Promoting Your Podcast

Here are some ideas for effectively promoting your podcast:

- Provide links to your podcasts on your website.
- Tell subscribers in your newsletter.
- Send an email blast to family, friends, colleagues, clients, and associates who might be impressed with how cool you are and pass the info on to their friends and associates.
- Use social media tools such as Facebook, Twitter, and LinkedIn.
- Participate in conversations on related websites, blogs, forums, chat rooms, discussion groups, and newsgroups; include a link to your podcast in the signature of all your posts.
- Create a press release to announce your show (see Chapter 12).
- Submit to iTunes. For directions on how to submit your podcast to iTunes, visit www.apple.com/itunes/podcasts/specs.html.

- Submit to Zune (www.zune.net). You'll need to download Zune's software, which is currently only available for Windows
- Submit to Blackberry (www.blackberry.com). It will be necessary to sign up for an account first.
- Submit to podcast search engines and directories (see next section).
- Submit to RSS directories (see Chapter 4, page 82).
- Submit podcast URL(s) to all the major search engines (Google, Yahoo!, Bing, and Dmoz).
- Place your podcast on Google Base (www.googlebase.com).
- Join associations, groups, and organizations in your field; attend meetings; and pass out CDs that contain "webisodes" of your podcast.
- Upload your podcast to YouTube along with an image by using the FREE tool found on MP32Tube (www.mp32tube.com).

FREE Podcast Directories

Submit your podcasts to ALL of the following search engines and directories (in addition to iTunes, Zune, and Blackberry):

iPodder (www.ipodder.org)
Podbean.com (www.podbean.com)
Podcast Pickle (www.podcastpickle.com)
Podcast.com (www.podcast.com)
Podcast Alley (www.podcastalley.com)
Podnova.Com (www.podnova.com)
Podseek (www.podseek.net)
The Podcast Network (www.thepodcastnetwork.com)

Chapter 11: Book Trailers and Videos

A book trailer is a great promotional tool that provides yet another way for people to find out about your book. Much like a movie trailer, a slick, well-produced, state-of-the-art multimedia video that combines graphics, text, music, animation, voice-over, and video effects in a compelling way allows you to tell the story of your book, highlighting its major benefits and bringing the whole drama to life.

It's very hard to talk about online video without mentioning YouTube. YouTube launched in 2005; it now commands over two billion views per day, nearly double the prime-time audience of all three major U.S. television broadcast networks combined. The site boasts over 260 million registered users, and it is estimated that the average person spends at least fifteen minutes per day on the site. The Queen of England even launched a YouTube channel back in 2007 (Good day, Ma'am, in case you're reading; and yes, I'm of British descent.)

Because of its huge popularity, YouTube is LOVED by Google. YouTube is one of the highest-ranking authority sites, which offers us yet another excellent SEO opportunity. YouTube allows you to upload both standard and high-definition video up to 2 gigabytes in size and no more than fifteen minutes in length. It accepts a wide variety of formats (simply converting files into the FLV format), including MPEG, AVI, MOV, and WMV files. When uploading a video, you have three fields in which to enter data: the title, description, and tags (or keywords) fields. These are the very fields that Google uses to rank your site. All three of these fields should be extremely descriptive and include your most important keywords as taken from your keyword list. Tagging your video properly means there is a good chance it will appear on the first page of Google search results, no matter how competitive your keywords are. Go ahead and say it...WOW!

You will also need to select the correct category for your video, so it can be found relatively easily. Current categories include the following:

- Autos and Vehicles
- Comedy
- Education
- Entertainment
- Film and Animation
- Gaming
- How-to and Style
- Music
- News and Politics
- Nonprofit and Activism
- People and Blogs
- Pets and Animals
- Science and Technology
- Sports
- Travel and Events

To convert a video viewer into a website visitor, place your site's URL (including "http://") at the beginning of the description field of ALL your videos as standard practice; YouTube converts these web addresses into active hyperlinks. Come up with creative, innovative ways to use video in your online promotional campaign that will help build your brand, drive targeted traffic to your website or blog, and generate book buzz. How about a series of how-to videos, live demonstrations, or creating a video log (or "vlog")? Because of our limited attention spans, a one- to two-minute video usually works best.

On YouTube, viewers have the opportunity to leave comments and ratings, share your content with other networks or social sites, subscribe to your channel, and tag their favorite videos. Regularly communicate with your viewers by responding to their comments. Receiving high scores from your audience will serve to further enhance your listings.

YouTube provides code that allows you to embed video into website pages. I embed my videos in my Media Room on my website, as it's like having a live ad (Oops! Did I say ad?) on the site. YouTube's embed function serves as a viral marketing tool because website and blog owners can also embed your video into their sites (once you enable the option) if they feel the information your book or video contains will be of value to their readers.

Note: YouTube lets you spread the word in real time by providing a link to your video upon upload that can be posted, shared, and viewed on your Facebook, Twitter, or Blogger accounts.

You can also be proactive and send your video to sites and blogs where you would like to have your book reviewed. It will be hard for them to resist the opportunity to showcase video along with a written or even an audio review. Online bookstores such as Amazon and Barnes & Noble also accept book trailers. Get reader interest and grab attention by featuring your multimedia content along with your book listing. It just adds a whole other dimension to the bookselling process.

So now that I've got you pumped, I know you're wondering where you can get a video made. I highly recommend the services offered by

Trailer to the Stars (www.trailertothestars.com). Specializing in multimedia marketing, Trailer to the Stars offers a wide range of video services, including professionally produced book trailer videos, speaker videos, and promotion videos. Executive producer Misty Taggart is an award-winning, twenty-year veteran Hollywood screenwriter whose staff members have produced numerous trailers for authors and therefore have a special understanding of our needs. Check the gallery that is displayed on the website, I'm sure you'll be impressed. And Misty has kindly agreed to extend a 10 percent discount to all readers.

Another way to get your video produced is to find enthusiastic, talented film students at a local college or university. Talk to staff in the career development office, ask to use their most gifted students, and make arrangements for them to receive extra credit for helping you out. You may also wish to enlist a friend or colleague who's handy with a video camera (which can be as simple as a cell phone with HD video recording capability) and familiar with computer software such as iMovie on the Mac or Windows Movie Maker, which comes preinstalled on the Windows platform. Whichever way you decide to go make sure you're reinforcing your brand and not detracting from your well-crafted online presence.

Note: To read an article entitled "Book Video Trailers: 11 Steps to Make Your Own," by Joanna Penn, visit The Creative Penn (bit.ly/jGmiJr).

Tip: For screen recording software, check ScreenFlow from Telestream (www.telestream.net) for the Mac, and Camtasia from TechSmith (www.techsmith.com) for Windows.

FREE Video Upload Services

Here is a list of FREE video upload services. All of them have different requirements and features, so check each one as needed. Keep your keyword list handy, as it will be necessary for you to associate tags with your video(s). I highly recommend that you upload your video(s) to your website or blog and to at least the first seven sites listed here.

YouTube (www.youtube.com)
Preview the Book (www.previewthebook.com)
Metacafe (www.metacafe.com)
SlideShare (www.slideshare.net)
sevenload (www.sevenload.com)
Vimeo (www.vimeo.com)
Revver (www.revver.com)
Viddler (www.viddler.com)
Graspr (www.graspr.com)
5min.com (www.5min.com)
MeFeedia (www.mefeedia.com)
Howcast (www.howcast.com)
Zoopy (www.zoopy.com)
VideoJug (www.videojug.com)
Flixya (www.flixya.com)

Tip: For our power users out there, TubeMogul (www.tubemogul.com) offers a video distribution and analytics service with price plans that start at $50 per month.

Chapter 12: Press Releases

The reason you're even reading this book is because you're quite aware that everything, and I mean everything, is somehow being migrated over to the Web–and that includes news. Just a few years ago, I would have told you to distribute your press release to journalists and editors at newspapers, magazines, and radio and TV stations by snail mail, fax, and email. Back then, we were at the mercy of these entities, but in today's environment, the old rules of marketing no longer apply. In fact, today we don't even create a press release with the "press" in mind. Why should we? With all due respect, we are no longer talking to the media. Now we talk directly to our target audience because if they think it's hot, then it really is news, and the press comes looking for us. How the tables have turned! POWER to the people!

A press release is simply an announcement that allows you to spread the word about your book. A press release can:

- Get free publicity for your book
- Generate media interest
- Increase book sales
- Help your target audience find you
- Drive targeted traffic to your website or blog

- Increase newsletter subscriptions
- Generate quality backlinks that help increase search engine rankings
- Increase brand awareness and visibility
- Increase exposure through viral marketing, as other publishers–who already have their own audiences–spread the news about your book by reprinting the contents of your release

Don't think of a press release as a one-time deal that you only create to announce the launch of your title. Find reasons to get in front of readers and create news as often as you can. Giving a lecture or seminar? Receiving an award? Creating a series of how-to videos or podcasts? Launching a related product or service? Developing an iPhone app? Hosting a webinar or an event? Contributing toward a charitable cause? These types of activities all deserve news announcements, as they relate to your book and bring further definition to your brand.

Tip: Set up a Google Alert (www.google.com/alerts) to receive a notification every time your press release is featured or referenced online.

Press Release Format

A press release should be written in the third person; have a clear, concise, attention-getting headline; and contain two to three brief paragraphs of about 400 words in total. Increase visibility and the possibility for a ton of new impressions for your book and your brand by following SEO techniques that include sprinkling keywords throughout the headline, subhead, and body of your text.

Although you'll be creating your press release primarily for online distribution, I suggest you create a one-pager in Microsoft Word using the standard, time-tested press release format. That way, you can easily create a PDF version that can be downloaded or displayed in HTML on your website. (I do both.) The format of your press release should be as follows:

Dateline

In the top left-hand margin, type the words "FOR IMMEDIATE RELEASE" in all caps. If you wish to release your news on or after a specific date, you can use the phrase "FOR RELEASE ON" and then include the date.

Media contact details

On the next lines, provide the contact information of the person to whom all inquiries should be directed. Include name, title, company name, address, phone number, fax number, email address, and company URL.

Headline

Your headline should be boldfaced, in all caps, and centered on the page. (Don't include exclamation points, as that's considered to be too "salesy.") Use it to instantly grab reader's attention. What are they looking for? What do they want or need the most? What is the ultimate benefit your book provides? Why is it newsworthy? What's so revolutionary about what you have written? Generate excitement by speaking to your readers on a personal level. Say, "Hey, this message is specially for you. I know exactly where you're coming from and what you need. I've got the answer." Inspire your readers with the hope that the advertised benefit can realistically be theirs. If you can do that, then they'll read on. Your headline should be catchy, clear, and concise. Think of it as a flashing billboard along the highway. What would you want to say in ten words or fewer? Make sure to use major keywords within the first four words. Ensure that your headline passes the "So what?" test.

Subhead

Elaborate on your headline, giving a little more information. This should be the bridge between your headline and the story, going a little deeper and better answering the question of what your book is about.

Make it no more than 200 characters long. A subhead is not always needed, but if you use one, center the text, use upper- and lowercase letters, and make the font slightly smaller than the headline. I like to use my subhead for testimonials I receive from notable figures.

Opening paragraph/Lead

Start with your location and the actual date (e.g., Atlanta, GA, December 12, 2012). This paragraph should summarize your book's information in such a way that if it were the only part of your press release that someone read, he or she would get the whole story. Include a hook–the one thing that gets people interested in reading on and possibly purchasing the title. Think about it from your readers' point of view, speak on their terms and in their language, and make sure to always address their "What's in it for me?" question.

Body

Use this section to back up the claims made in your headline, subhead, and opening paragraph. Expand on the benefit(s) of your book by going into more detail. If you can, for a personal touch, try to include quotes or testimonials from reviewers, readers, subject matter experts, or even yourself as the author.

Final paragraph

Restate and summarize the key points of your press release, give your final thoughts, and close out.

Boilerplate

Provide purchasing information as follows:

- Book title (including the subtitle)
- Author's name
- Any relevant credentials (certification, awards, industry recognition)
- Other relevant publications

- Release date
- ISBN
- Price
- Publishing company
- Website
- Ordering information (wholesalers, retailers, online outlets, etc.)

Close

Indicate the end of your release by using the standard "###" symbol (minus the quotes) centered at the bottom of the page.

Tip: In the boilerplate section, you may want to include extra information such as whether there are review copies available; where excerpts can be viewed or downloaded online; and whether the author is available for speaking engagements, bookings, or interviews.

FREE Press Release Distribution Services

Just perform a Google search for "free press release distribution" to come up with a ton of sites that offer this service. This section includes the ones I have personally used and can vouch for. My release was republished all over the Web (including www.usatoday.com); it received high Google rankings; I got numerous interview requests and even an offer for an appearance on a major television network; and if that wasn't enough, I also noticed an increase in traffic to my website. It's truly amazing what you can do for FREE online, and your press release will exist in cyberspace for a very long time, if not forever.

You may consider paying a small fee to upgrade your account. This will allow you to access additional features such as the ability to include graphics, embed clickable links in the body of your release, and have your release distributed through that particular company's RSS feed. At a minimum, you should create accounts with and submit your press release to each and every one of the following FREE services:

1888PressRelease (www.1888pressrelease.com)
24-7 Press Release (www.24-7pressrelease.com)
BigNews.biz (www.bignews.biz)
Free Press Release (www.free-press-release.com)
iNewswire (www.inewswire.com)
Newswire Today (www.newswiretoday.com)
PR.com (www.pr.com)
PressBox (www.pressbox.co.uk)
PRLog (www.prlog.org)
PR Urgent (www.prurgent.com)

Chapter 13: Industry Reviews

It's a fact that great reviews sell books. To build credibility and boost online promotion efforts (e.g., on Amazon, your author site, blog, press release, etc.), you should aim to get reviews from some of the most trusted and reputable sources in the publishing industry. Although reviews do not have much to do with SEO, they have everything to do with increased exposure, as information about your title gets published on the reviewers' websites, in their print magazines, on forums, and in some cases even propagated to all the major book databases around the world. Booksellers and librarians rely on the information from these industry leaders when making purchasing decisions, and reviews provide you with an opportunity to get in front of these book-buying eyes.

Because of the number of submissions these organizations receive, coverage is not guaranteed or automatic. Check each review organization's website to find particular submission guidelines. Some accept book (or galley) submissions prior to publication; others accept books only after publication. Some accept electronic submissions; others don't. Make sure to check what the particular requirements are.

I've been lucky enough to receive reviews from a number of the organizations listed in this chapter. When submitting, I include a cover letter, media kit, bookmarks, flyers, and any other promotional materials I have. Along with these items, I submit a galley, or uncorrected proof, that I have printed up at either Lulu (www.lulu.com) or Blurb (www.blurb.com), depending on the particular requirements of the project.

As you will notice, all of the reviewers request different publication information details. To handle this, I send a summary of information, along with a press kit. Here is an example of the information I might send to reviewers for this book. I would include this information on my cover letter as well as on the first printed page inside the book:

360 Books Presents For Review

Uncorrected galley proof. To be used for review purposes only.
Do not quote without prior permission from the publisher.

Category: Internet marketing/Reference books–Publishing
Title: Online Book Marketing: The Least Expensive, Most Effective Ways to Create Book Buzz
Author: Lorraine Phillips
ISBN: 978-0-9822765-5-6
LCCN: 2011920158
Publication date: 6/11
Price: $21.95
Number of pages: 224
Trim size: 6" x 9"
Binding: Perfect-bound
Cover type: Paperback only
Distributor: Ingram

Publicity contact: Karen Thornson
Phone/fax: 1-800-360-2012
Email: kthornson@3sixtybooks.com

Publisher: 360 Books, LLC
Address: PO Box 105603, #22430, Atlanta, GA 30348-5603
Phone/fax: 1-800-360-2012
Email: galley@3sixtybooks.com
Website: www.3sixtybooks.com

NOT FOR RESALE.

Book Review Company Information

Although there are many review companies you can submit to (some for a fee), this section lists the pertinent information for the most prominent and respected book reviewing companies within the industry. All of these reputable companies review your publication for FREE, except for *ForeWord* Digital Reviews, where there is a $129 fee if your book is accepted for a digital review. To increase your chances of receiving a review send your publication to ALL the appropriate companies listed below.

Name: *Booklist Online*
Description: *Booklist* is a 100-year-old journal published by the American Library Association, whose core mission is to provide public and school librarians with reviews that help them decide what to buy.
URL: www.booklistonline.com/GeneralInfo.aspx?id=65
Directions: Two galley copies should be sent at least fifteen weeks prior to publication. In cases where no galleys are available, *Booklist* accepts a photocopied manuscript, page proofs, folded and gathered sheets, or other forms of prepublication copy. Galleys received fewer than fifteen weeks before publication will be considered, provided they are sent to *Booklist* before they are sent to *Publishers Weekly, Kirkus Reviews*, and *Library Journal.* Review copies must include a publication slip specifying prices and ISBNs for all editions, publication date (month and year), and publisher/distributor information. Any publisher of a book accepted for review by *Booklist* will receive a tear sheet of the review.
Mailing Address: *Booklist*, American Library Association, 50 E. Huron St., Chicago, IL 60611

Name: *Choice* Magazine
Description: A magazine of the American Library Association, *Choice* provides reviews for academic libraries. Nearly 7,000 reviews are published annually, spanning all academic disciplines.

URL: www.ala.org/ala/mgrps/divs/acrl/publications/choice/infoforpub/informationpublishers.cfm
Directions: Submit finished copies of books or full versions (no demo copies) of electronic media. *Choice* does not review galleys or uncorrected proofs. For each title, include publication date, distributor information, price, and ISBN. No review will be published without a price in U.S. dollars.
Mailing Address: CHOICE, 575 Main St., Suite 300, Middletown, CT 06457-3445

Name: *ForeWord Reviews*
Description: The readership of *ForeWord* magazine is composed of 20,000 librarians, booksellers, publishing professionals, and other book lovers who require a reliable source of reviews of independent and university presses. *ForeWord* offers two types of reviews: (1) *ForeWord Reviews* print magazine and (2) *ForeWord* Digital Reviews ($129) for an online review if the title is unable to be covered in the magazine. All reviews (both print and online) are featured on the *ForeWord* website and licensed for publication in the top title information databases used by booksellers and librarians: Baker & Taylor's TitleSource 3, Ingram's iPage, Bowker's Books in Print, and Gale's licensed databases.
URL: www.forewordreviews.com/get-reviewed/submission-guidelines/
Directions: For hardcopy ARCs and galleys, submit one copy of the book, along with a press release or a fact sheet that summarizes why the title is distinctive and different and contains the following information:

- Category
- Title
- Subtitle
- Author
- Publisher
- Number of illustrations
- Pages

- Prices
- Binding
- ISBNs of formats
- Publication dates
- Publisher's name, address, phone, and fax

For electronic submissions, send a query, fact sheet, cover art, and the first three chapters of the book. Send queries to heather@forewordmagazine.com.
Mailing Address: Book Review Editor at *ForeWord Reviews*, 129 1/2 East Front St., Traverse City, MI 49684

Name: *Independent Publisher*
Description: *Independent Publisher* is a trade journal for the independent publishing community, specializing in marketing and promotion for independent authors and publishers. IP Online publishes new title listings of books released by independent, university, and self-publishers, to bring increased recognition to the thousands of great, and often overlooked, independently published titles released each year.
URL: www.independentpublisher.com/highlighted-submit.php
Directions: Submit one copy of a bound galley, finished book, ebook, or audiobook. Send books prior to publication date if possible and within ninety days past the publication date at the latest. Submitted books must include a cover sheet with the following information: title, author, publisher, address, phone, website, distributor (if any), page count, cover style, price, ISBN, publication month and year.
Follow-Up: Send a follow-up email to Jim Barnes at jimb@bookpublishing.com to confirm receipt of your title. Include a cover scan (72 dpi; 2 inches wide) and book synopsis (150–250 words) to make it easier to complete your listing.
Mailing Address: Jim Barnes, Independent Publisher Online, Highlighted Title Listings, 1129 Woodmere Ave., Suite B, Traverse City, MI 49686

Name: *Kirkus Reviews*
Description: *Kirkus Reviews* is a powerful resource for millions of readers, writers, librarians, media executives, and the publishing industry.
URL: www.kirkusreviews.com/about/submission-guidlines
Directions: *Kirkus Reviews* considers any previously unpublished titles that are submitted in galley or manuscript form (galleys preferred) at least three to four months before publication date. Two galley copies are required. Two copies of the finished book are required once available. Include information such as price; publication date (the more exact, the better); ISBN; page count; as well as a brief description of the book and some particulars about the author.
Mailing Address:
Adult fiction: Elaine Szewczyk, Kirkus Reviews, 1133 Broadway, Suite 406, New York, NY 10010
Adult nonfiction: Eric Liebetrau, Kirkus Reviews, 479 Old Carolina Ct., Mt. Pleasant, SC 29464
Children's and young adult: Vicky Smith, Kirkus Reviews, 99 Mitchell Rd., South Portland, ME 04106

Name: *Library Journal* (LJ)
Description: In its 133rd year of publication, *Library Journal* is the oldest and most respected publication covering the library field. Considered to be the bible of the library world, LJ is read by over one hundred thousand library directors, administrators, and staff in public, academic, and special libraries. Review sections evaluate nearly 7,000 books annually, along with hundreds of audiobooks, videos, databases, websites, and systems that libraries buy.
URL: www.libraryjournal.com/csp/cms/sites/LJ/SubmitToLJ/TitlesForReview.csp
Directions: Provide one copy of the galley, proofs, or manuscript three to four months in advance of publication date. Finished books should be sent as early as possible with the words "In Lieu of Galleys." Include the following: author; book title; name, address, and telephone

number of publisher; date of publication; price; number of pages; and ISBN and LC numbers if available. Indicate whether illustrations, an index, or a bibliography is included; also include a brief description of the book, its intended audience, and information on the author's background.
Follow-Up: Send an email to LJBookReview@reedbusiness.com
Mailing Address: Book Review Editor, Library Journal, 160 Varick St., 11th Floor, New York, NY 10013

Name: *Midwest Book Review* (MBR)
Description: *The Midwest Book Review* is a major Internet resource for publishers, writers, librarians, booksellers, and book lovers of all ages and interests. MBR publishes monthly reviews specifically designed for community and academic librarians, booksellers, and the general reading public. Reviews are posted on several thematically appropriate websites, databases, online discussion groups, and Internet bookstores such as Amazon. MBR gives priority consideration to small press publishers, self-published authors, and academic presses.
URL: www.midwestbookreview.com/get_rev.htm
Directions: Submit two finished copies of the book (no galleys or uncorrected proofs). Include a cover letter and a publicity release or media kit.
Mailing Address: James A. Cox, Editor-in-chief, Midwest Book Review, 278 Orchard Dr., Oregon, WI 53575
Name: *Publishers Weekly*
Description: *Publishers Weekly* is the book industry's leading news magazine (print and digital versions), covering every aspect of creating, producing, marketing, and selling the written word in book, audio, video, and electronic formats. Since 1872, *Publishers Weekly* has delivered in-depth interviews with top authors and publishers, detailed reports on industry issues and trends, and over 7,000 book and media reviews each year.
URL: www.publishersweekly.com/pw/corp/submissionguidelines.html

Directions: Submissions should be sent three to four months prior to publication. Send two copies of every title submitted, as single-copy submissions will not be considered. Finished books and bound manuscripts are acceptable for submission. Clearly mark them "In Lieu of Galleys." Unbound folded and gathered pages (F & Gs) are acceptable only for submission of heavily illustrated books. All galleys should have the following information on the cover:

- Title
- Author
- Price
- Publisher and imprint
- Format
- Number of pages in the finished book
- 13-digit ISBN
- Month and day of publication
- Distribution arrangements
- Publicity contact information

An accompanying letter should contain a description or synopsis of the book and any pertinent publicity information, including the author's previous titles, blurbs, or previous reviews. Book club, paperback, audio, or movie rights sales; author tours of five cities or more; a print run of more than 10,000; or an ad/promo budget of more than $30,000 should be noted.

Mailing Address:

Nonfiction reviews (or "Poetry Reviews" or other relevant category): Publishers Weekly Nonfiction Reviews, 71 West 23 St. #1608, New York, NY 10010

Religious titles: Marcia Z. Nelson, Publishers Weekly Religion Reviews, 1118 Garfield St., Aurora, IL 60506

Children's book submissions: Children's Book Reviews, Publishers Weekly, 71 West 23 St. #1608, New York, NY 10010

Name: *School Library Journal* (SLJ)
Description: *School Library Journal* serves librarians who work with students in school and public libraries. SLJ reaches an audience of more than one hundred thousand. The world's largest and most authoritative reviewer of children's and young adult content–principally books, but also audio, video, and the Web–the magazine and its website provide 38,000 subscribers with information indispensable in making purchasing decisions. *School Library Journal* reviews new children's and young adult general trade books, original paperbacks, and reference books from established publishers and does NOT review books that are either self-published or directly submitted by authors.
URL: www.schoollibraryjournal.com/csp/cms/sites/SLJ/Info/submissions.csp
Directions: Two copies of the book must be received at least two months prior to publication. Galleys may be submitted; however, they must be followed by two copies of the finished book. Submitted titles should include the following bibliographic information: author, title, binding(s), price(s), publication month and year, ISBN(s), Library of Congress number (or notice that there will not be one), and whether Cataloging in Publication data will appear in the book.
Mailing Address: SLJ Book Review, *School Library Journal,* 160 Varick St., 11th Floor, New York, NY 10013

Chapter 14:
Industry Awards

If you wouldn't mind the title of "Award-Winning Author," then this final chapter is just for you. Prestige as an author is one of the many benefits of winning a distinguished book award from a highly respected organization in the publishing industry. Having this seal of approval means that you have been recognized and honored for exhibiting editorial excellence. What an endorsement! The credibility this brings allows you to command the attention of the media, reviewers, distributors, bloggers, and book buyers alike, giving you the ultimate exposure you need to... well...sell more books. Here is a list of recognized organizations that give book and/or design awards. Good luck with submissions, and please let me know if there are any winners in the crowd!

ForeWord Reviews' Book of the Year Awards
URL: www.forewordreviews.com/services/book-of-the-year-awards
Entry Fee: $75 per title, per category
Description: *ForeWord Reviews'* Book of the Year Awards were established to bring increased attention to librarians and booksellers of the literary and graphic achievements of independent publishers and their authors. *ForeWord* is the only review trade journal devoted exclusively to books from independent houses. Finalists are determined

by a jury of judges consisting of editors and reviewers of *ForeWord Reviews*, booksellers, librarians, and other industry professionals. Decisions are based on editorial excellence, professional production, originality of the narrative, author credentials relative to the book, and the value the book adds to its genre. First-, second-, and third-place winners will be awarded in each category. A $1,500 cash prize will also be awarded to Best Fiction and Best Nonfiction as determined by the editors of *ForeWord Reviews*.

IBPA Benjamin Franklin Awards
URL: www.thebenjaminfranklinawards.com
Entry Fee: IBPA member – $90 per title, per category; Non-IBPA member – $190 for first title, which includes one year's membership in IBPA, and $90 per title, per category for second and subsequent entries
Description: IBPA Benjamin Franklin Awards recognize excellence in both editorial and design and are regarded as one of the highest national honors in small and independent publishing. Finalists and winners receive award certificates, along with gold or silver stickers. All winners and finalists are announced to the major trade journals and media. In addition, finalists are featured on the IBPA's home page prior to the event, and winners and finalists remain archived at the IBPA website. Award winners are recognized at the IBPA booth at BookExpo America and displayed in a designated location on a space-available basis. All entrants receive critique sheets with advice on how to improve their publications. There are fifty-six categories.

***Independent Publisher* "IPPY" Book Awards**
URL: www.independentpublisher.com/ipland/IPAwards.php
Entry Fee: $75–$95 for a national entry, depending on submission date; $75–$95 for a regional-only entry, depending on submission date. The fee to add a regional entry is $45.

Description: *Independent Publisher* Book Awards honor the best independently published titles. The awards are intended to bring increased recognition to the thousands of exemplary independent, university, and self-published titles published each year, rewarding those who exhibit the courage, innovation, and creativity to bring about change in the world of publishing. The contest is open to independent authors and publishers worldwide who produce books written in English that are intended for the North American market. Judging is based on content, originality, design, and production quality, with emphasis on innovation and social relevance. All announced medalists in the national and regional categories will receive gold, silver, or bronze medals and personalized certificates; Outstanding Books of the Year will receive gold medals and certificates. Metallic foil seals will be available to all medalists in their appropriate award levels. Awards are presented at the BookExpo America ceremony or mailed to those unable to attend. Publicity includes the awards event, a media blitz, and yearlong exposure at *Independent Publisher* Online (www.independentpublisher.com) and various publishing and bookselling websites.

Indie Book Awards

URL: www.indiebookawards.com

Entry Fee: $75 per title for the first category entered; $50 fee for each additional title

Description: The Indie Book Awards are presented by the Independent Book Publishing Professionals Group. The group accepts submissions from all indie book authors and publishers, including independent publishers (small, medium, or otherwise), university presses, self-published authors, ebook authors, seasoned authors, and even first-time authors, in the United States, Canada, or internationally who have a book that is written in English. There are sixty categories to choose from, and the awards are as follows:

Best Fiction Book: $1,500 cash prize and trophy
Best Nonfiction Book: $1,500 cash prize and trophy
Second Best Fiction Book: $750 cash prize and trophy
Second Best Nonfiction Book: $750 cash prize and trophy
Third Best Fiction Book: $500 cash prize and trophy
Third Best Nonfiction Book: $500 cash prize and trophy
Best Design Book: $250 cash prize and trophy
The winner of each of the sixty categories: $100 cash prize and gold medal
Finalist medals will be awarded to up to three finalists in each of the sixty categories.

The National Book Awards (The National Book Foundation)
URL: www.nationalbook.org/nbaentry.html
Entry Fee: $125 for each title submitted
Description: The Foundation will announce a finalist short list of the five outstanding books submitted in each category of Fiction, Nonfiction, Poetry, and Young People's Literature. One winner in each genre receives $10,000 for the best book chosen in Fiction, Nonfiction, Poetry, and Young People's Literature. Sixteen short list prizes of $1,000 each will be awarded to the finalists. Must be a U.S. citizen to apply.

The National Indie Excellence Book Awards
URL: www.indieexcellence.com
Entry Fee: $69 per entry, per category
Description: Indie Excellence is open to all English-language books that are available for sale both online and off. Entries must be books in print, including small presses, midsize independent publishers, university presses, and self-published authors. All titles must have an ISBN and be published books. Winners and finalists will be listed on IndieExcellence.com and will be included in a news release announcement of the winners. Various other sponsor choice prizes are also awarded.

Reader Views Literary Awards

URL: www.readerviews.com/Awards.html

Entry Fee: $75–$85 per title, depending on submission date; $20 for each additional category or regional/global entry

Description: These annual literary awards were established to honor writers who self-published or had their books published by a subsidy publisher, small press, university press, or independent book publisher geared for the North American reading audience. POD books are accepted. Three finalists will be chosen in each Fiction and Nonfiction category. First- and second-place winners will be awarded in each category. Third place will receive an honorable mention. One finalist, the top score in each area, will be chosen in each regional and global category. Each winner receives a certificate of recognition.

Writer's Digest Self-Published Book Awards

URL: www.writersdigest.com/selfpublished

Entry Fee: $125 for the first entry; $75 for each additional entry

Description: *Writer's Digest* is looking for the best self-published books. The grand prize winner is awarded $3,000 cash and promotion in *Writer's Digest* and *Publishers Weekly*. The editors of *Writer's Digest* will endorse and submit ten copies of the grand prize-winning book to major review houses such as *The New York Times* and *The Washington Post*. In addition, Book Marketing Works, LLC, will provide a one-year membership in Publishers Marketing Association; guaranteed acceptance in a special-sales catalog, providing national representation through 5,000 salespeople selling to nonbookstore markets; guaranteed acceptance by Atlas Books (a top distributor to wholesalers, chains, independents, and online retailers); and six hours of book shepherding from Poynter Book Shepherd, Ellen Reid. In addition, they also select ten first-place winners and honorable mention winners. All other entrants receive a certificate of participation; a brief judge's commentary; and a listing with a link on the *Writer's Digest* site, provided an accurate URL is submitted.

Appendix A:
Questions to Ask Your Web Designer or Web Design Firm

Is there an online portfolio I can view?

Most designers showcase completed projects online. Make sure you like the work presented and use the web faux pas checklist on page 45 to evaluate a prospective designer's level of competency.

Will you be working from a template, or will it be an original design?

Because of your specific needs, a designer will probably suggest that you go with an original design. A template-based site, however, can be updated and customized according to your particular requirements. Request quotes for both. If developing a WordPress site, then it will be easy enough to hunt down a theme that you can have customized for your brand.

Can you implement newsletter sign-up, survey, and contact form scripts?

Scripts should be set up to accept and process any data or correspondence you receive from your site and notifications sent to you via email.

How long will it take to complete the design?

This will depend on the complexity of the project and your designer's anticipated workload at the time.

What information will I need to provide?

Get clear direction on the information you will need to provide your designer with. Define your number of pages and the title of each. What text do you need to supply? Will you also be supplying graphics, videos, or MP3's? Make sure all the specifics are outlined and well documented so as not to slow down the process. Also, please know that you are responsible for the accuracy of the information you supply; it is not your designer's job to correct spelling or fix bad grammar.

What will be the approximate cost?

Submit requests to at least three designers for price comparison. Even better, if you use an online freelance provider service, designers will bid at competitive prices for your project.

What are the payment terms?

All design shops function differently, but you will receive a proposal or estimate that is usually valid for thirty days, based on the project specifications and the anticipated scope of the work. When you approve and sign off on the estimate, you will need to deposit 50 percent of the total, with the balance due upon prototype sign-off as discussed below.

What forms of payment do you accept?

Credit card, PayPal, certified check? Find out in advance so that you can be prepared.

What is the usual development process? What checkpoints and milestones will there be along the way?

After you sign off on the estimate, pay the deposit, and supply your designer with all the necessary information and documentation needed for your project, he or she will create either a prototype web page, a sketch, or a printout that demonstrates the general page layout of your site. In the case of a prototype, actual functionality will not be implemented until later on in the process. The design will demonstrate the colors, fonts, navigation, buttons, logo and graphics placement, and any other design-related elements pertinent to the project.

You will work together to refine the design until you have something you are satisfied with. At this point, you will give your approval for the designer to continue the work to completion. When the designer has completed the design, then you will work together again, changing and refining as necessary until you are satisfied with the results. At that time, you will sign off to indicate that the project is complete.

What happens if I do not like the design?

If, as you work with your designer to refine the design, you just can't seem to see eye to eye and he or she seems incapable of implementing your ideas, then it will be necessary for you to cut ties and pay the money owed thus far. If you take time to find a designer who comes with a recommendation, matches your style, and has produced work you are impressed with, this scenario should not arise.

What happens if I decide to cancel the project?

This will depend on how far along in the process you are when you decide to cancel the project. Charges for services rendered may be 25 percent to 50 percent if the work is canceled during the initial design phase, 50 percent if canceled after the completion and sign-off on the prototype, and 100 percent if canceled after the final design is complete.

How are revisions and alterations handled along the way?

If the revisions or alterations are deemed in scope, according to the original proposal, then they are already included as part of the estimated fee. If developments require new items or functionality that are deemed out of scope, then a new proposal and estimate will have to be generated.

How is website compatibility testing handled? What browsers and platforms do you test on?

Your website should be tested to ensure it acts and looks the same regardless of platform, operating system, browser, or device used. At a minimum, insist that your site be tested on both Mac and PC and a couple mobile devices as well as in various browsers including Firefox, Internet Explorer, Opera, and Safari.

How will the completed site be delivered and in what format?

Your designer can simply upload your files to your server, which in essence makes your site go live. He or she can also opt to send you a copy of the files via email or, depending on size, pop a CD into the mail.

Will you provide tech support? If so, for how long?

Most designers will offer FREE technical support for anywhere from seven to thirty days after your site goes live, providing an opportunity to work out any minor quirks, bugs, or tweaks. Use this period to thoroughly go through your site to ensure it functions and displays exactly as expected.

Will I be able to handle site updates myself?

The answer to this question will vary according to what solution your designer decides to implement for you and what web skills you possess. If this option is important to you then say so at the onset of the project in order to make the designer aware of your needs. With content management systems such as WordPress and Drupal that allow for easy updating by non–tech savvy users, this may not be a problem.

If you are not using a content management system such as WordPress or Drupal, and you are not particularly that tech-savvy, then you are advised to check into a product offered by Adobe called Contribute (available for both Mac and PC). Contribute allows nontechnical folks to quickly and easily edit website content directly from their browser window. Its interface and functionality are very similar to that of Microsoft Word, so if you can use Word, then you can use this too.

How will you handle site updates and maintenance? How much will you charge for these services?

If you will not be handling the site updates yourself, then you have a couple of options. You can either pay the charge for each update as it occurs, or if you anticipate regular updates to your site, you can purchase a web maintenance agreement with a monthly fee for a set number of hours that your site will be worked on every month. If the entire amount is not used up within a month, then most designers will allow the remaining charges to be rolled over into the following month. If, on the other hand, you go over the time allocated for a given month, you will be charged at a discounted hourly rate for the additional time spent updating and maintaining you site.

Appendix B: Essential WordPress Plug-ins

Here is a list of essential WordPress plug-ins, suggested by WordPress guru Ken Dawes, also known as "The Web Mechanic" (www.the-web-mechanic.com). Find him on Twitter @thewebmechanic.

Security

Because of WordPress's popularity and widespread use, the software provides an attractive target to hackers. You can do a lot to bulletproof your WordPress installation, with the following plug-ins providing the most bang for your buck.

Akismet

Although it comes standard with all WordPress installations, it has to be set up and activated. This tool helps combat comment spam.

Block Bad Queries (BBQ)

BBQ secures WordPress against hacker attacks.

Growmap Anti-Spambot Plug-in (G.A.S.P.)

This plug-in all but eliminates comment spam by placing a checkbox on the comment submission form that spambots are unable to check off.

Login LockDown

This protects your login form so that after three incorrect login attempts, you are banned from logging in for an hour. Many attackers will try thousands of passwords in an attempt to break into your site, but this essential plug-in will stop them in their tracks.

WordPress Antivirus

This antivirus protection for your blog protects against malicious spam and code injections.

WordPress Firewall 2

WordPress Firewall 2 provides protection against malicious attacks on your WordPress site.

WordPress Hashcash

WordPress Hashcash eradicates spam sign-ups on WordPress sites. This plug-in can be used in conjunction with Akismet.

Search Engine Optimization (SEO)

Remember, the three most important things for SEO are content, content, and content! The following are a few of the plug-ins that can assist you with best SEO practices.

All in One SEO Pack, Platinum SEO Pack, or HeadSpace2

There are a multitude of SEO plug-ins available for WordPress, but these three are the most popular. More recently, I have been leaning toward HeadSpace2. It's more of an effort to set up, but it is like a Swiss Army knife in its versatility and capabilities. HeadSpace2 includes an amazing number of options such as built-in Google Analytics support. For a simpler plug-in, go with the Platinum SEO Pack.

Google XML Sitemaps

This plug-in adds a sitemap that enables search engines to better index your site.

Ultimate Google Analytics

This plug-in adds Google Analytics to your site with numerous options.

Miscellaneous

Blubrry PowerPress Podcasting Plug-in

This plug-in seamlessly adds the features necessary to extend a WordPress blog to a podcasting engine.

FeedBurner FeedSmith

This Google plug-in connects your WordPress RSS feed to Google's FeedBurner service. FeedBurner allows you to keep statistics on the people subscribing to your RSS feed and allows your subscribers to receive your postings via email as well.

NextGEN Gallery

NextGEN Gallery does just about everything you'd ever want to do with images over and above the basics offered by WordPress.

TinyMCE Advanced

This plug-in adds many features to the standard WordPress editor, including the ability to compose a blog post in MS Word and then copy and paste it into WordPress. Not using this plug-in can cause problems in WordPress, as Word adds hidden coding that can mess up the format of a post.

Appendix C:
100 Subject Line Spam Filter Triggers

Spam triggers are words or combinations of words used in the subject line of emails that have been identified as the most commonly used terms for spam messages. Internet service providers analyze incoming emails and use a point system to cut down on or block spam according to certain trigger words found within subject lines. If your email is deemed as having too many points, then it will likely be rerouted to the recipient's junk mail folder or be filtered out altogether, never even reaching your subscriber. The following is a list of 100 spam filter triggers that you should avoid using within your email subject header line.

1. #1
2. $$$
3. 100% free
4. 100% satisfied
5. 50% off!
6. Ad
7. Affordable
8. All natural

9. Apply now
10. Apply online
11. As seen on...
12. As seen on Oprah
13. Best price
14. Billion
15. Buy direct
16. Call now!
17. Cash bonus
18. Cheap
19. Claims
20. Click here
21. Collect child support
22. Congratulations
23. Consolidate your debt
24. Credit
25. Discount
26. Discount!
27. Double your income
28. Earn $
29. Easy terms
30. Eliminate debt
31. Email marketing
32. Extra income
33. Fast cash
34. Financial freedom
35. Financially independent
36. Free
37. Free gift
38. Free membership
39. Free offer
40. Full refund
41. Get it now

42. Get paid
43. Guarantee
44. Home-based
45. Home-based business
46. Increase traffic
47. Increase your sales
48. Incredible deal
49. Information you requested
50. Info you requested
51. Legal
52. Lose weight
53. Lower interest rates
54. Lower monthly payment
55. Mail in order form
56. Make $
57. Marketing
58. Million dollars
59. Money back
60. Month trial offer
61. Mortgage rates
62. No catch
63. No cost, no fees
64. No credit check
65. No gimmicks
66. No hidden costs
67. No obligation
68. No purchase necessary
69. No questions asked
70. Offer expires
71. One time
72. One-time
73. Online marketing
74. Order

75. Order now
76. Order status
77. Order today
78. Please read
79. Potential earnings
80. Preapproved
81. Prices
82. Print out and fax
83. Promise You
84. Refinance
85. Remove
86. Reverses Aging
87. Risk free
88. Satisfaction guaranteed
89. Solutions
90. Special promotion
91. Stop snoring
92. Subscribe
93. Success
94. Thousands
95. Unsecured debt or credit
96. Urgent
97. While supplies last
98. Work at home
99. You're a winner!
100. You've been selected

Onlinebookbuzz.com

To access all the links and resources presented in this book, please visit www.onlinebookbuzz.com. Click "Links" from the navigation menu and enter the following username and password:

username: myplatform
password: love2.0

Glossary

"Alt" attribute: The text description of an image that is displayed when a mouse hovers over it.

Anchor text: The visible text (that usually appears underlined and in blue) on a web page that connects to either another web page, a graphic, a download, or another section of the page. When hovering over a clickable link, the cursor changes into a hand pointer icon.

Ancillary products: A product or service an author can sell, in addition to his or her book, to raise brand awareness and generate additional income.

Animation: A simulation of movement created by displaying a series of independent pictures or frames.

Article marketing: Content-driven marketing in which an individual or a business writes short, information-based articles related to their specific industry and makes those articles available for publication and syndication to increase credibility and attract business or clients.

Article marketing directories: Directories where you can submit articles for publication, syndication, and increased exposure.

Atom feed: Allows you to syndicate or distribute headlines from your blog, podcast, or website to a web feed.

Attribute: Refers to the properties that supply additional information about an HTML element. For instance, the <img> tag is used to display an image on a web page and can have various attributes, such as height, width, border size, border color, etc. For a real-world example, if a tag were a dress suit, then the attributes could be blue color, wool fabric, medium size, and gold buttons.

Attribution: Giving full credit to and providing information on the author or creator of an article, photograph, musical score, podcast, or other media.

Authority site: A popular site that is frequently visited, contains large amounts of strong content, has numerous incoming links based on merit and relevance, and is often referred to as a trusted source. Amazon.com, Wikipedia.com, and YouTube.com are all examples of authority sites.

Author platform: The activities performed by an author to connect with readers. Can consist of attracting people to sign up for a mailing list, participating in social media networks, having a web presence, blogging, public speaking, holding seminars or workshops, hosting a show or podcast, or appearing on radio and television.

Autoresponder: Computer software or configuration that automatically responds to an email it receives.

Backlinks: Incoming links to a website or web page.

Black hat SEO: Unethical and unacceptable search engine optimization practices that are not approved of by search engine companies.

Blacklist: A database of Internet addresses, or IPs, known to be used by spammers and denied a particular privilege, service, access, or recognition.

Blog (or web log)**:** An interactive website that functions as an online diary where you can publish your thoughts; share your views, ideas, and opinions; discuss issues; divulge information; give advice; report on breaking news; provide useful links, photos, and videos; or share your expertise and knowledge on a particular subject.

Blogger: A person who writes, publishes, and updates a blog.

Blogging: The act of writing, publishing, and updating a blog.

Blogroll: A list of blogs recommended by a blogger, which usually appears as a sidebar menu on a blog site.

Body text: The main, readable text contained on a web page.

Book trailer: A promotional video advertisement for a book that functions much like a movie trailer, combining graphics, text, music, animation, voice-over, and video effects.

Bounced email: An email that cannot be delivered to a recipient's inbox for some reason and is instead sent back (or bounced back) to the sender with an error message.

Brand: The specific identity of a product, service, or business.

Browser incompatibility: When a website displays incorrectly depending on the browser, browser version, platform, or device it is being viewed on.

Byline: The author's name and brief bio information that accompany an article or story.

Chat room: An online community that gives users a way to communicate with one another and discuss general topics of interest.

Clickable link: A graphic or a portion of text (that usually appears underlined and in blue) on a web page that connects to either another web page, a graphic, a download, or another section of the same document in which the link appears. When hovering over a clickable link, the cursor changes into a hand pointer icon.

Click path: This web statistic shows the actual path a visitor takes while browsing a website.

CMYK: The four ink colors used for printing, namely cyan (blue), magenta (red), yellow, and black. The four inks are combined in different quantities to reproduce and print almost all colors. Also known as four color or process color.

Contact form: An online form that sends out content over email without the need to physically display an email address, which can easily be harvested by spammers.

Content: The information or readable text presented on a website or in other media.

Content management system (CMS)**:** Computer software or system used for organizing, managing, storing, and facilitating the creation of documents and other digital assets. Systems can be either online or offline. Blogging software such as WordPress is an example of an online content management system.

Control panel: The graphical interface provided by a web hosting company that is used to control or administer a site.

Conversion rate: The rate at which a casual visitor to a website either is converted into a customer or takes some type of desired action, such as making a purchase, signing up for a newsletter, subscribing to an RRS feed, or downloading a white paper.

Copyright: Protects original works of authorship from use without permission. Copyright can be assigned to published and unpublished works.

Copyright infringement: The use of a copyrighted work, in whole or in part, without the original copyright holder's permission.

Crawler: An automated software program that scans the Web with the purpose of storing and indexing web page information for search engine results.

CSS (cascading style sheets)**:** A style language that defines the format and layout of an HTML document.

Demographic information: Statistical data relating to a particular group within the population. Can include information such as age, income, and attained level of education.

Design: The art of visual communication, utilizing color, type, illustration, photography, and layout techniques to present content or information that communicates effectively and is aesthetically pleasing to the eye.

Discussion board: An online community that gives users a way to communicate with one another and discuss general topics of interest.

Domain name: The "human-friendly" identification label or address of a website on the Internet.

Double opt-in: A process where an email address must be confirmed before being officially added to a subscription database list.

Email blast: An electronic mailing sent out to a large mailing list.

Email marketing: A form of direct and content-driven marketing in which messages are distributed and communicated over email to an opt-in list of subscribers.

Exit page: A web statistic that shows the last page visited by a reader before leaving a website.

Facebook (www.facebook.com)**:** The number one social networking site with over 500 million active users that connects friends, family, professionals, and businesses from around the world. Facebook was founded in 2004 by Harvard student Mark Zuckerberg, and was originally named thefacebook.

Facebook Groups: As found on Facebook.com and used for businesses and brands that wish to build communities that connect people within a certain industry for discussion and informational purposes. Groups can be set as public or private.

Facebook Pages: As found on Facebook.com and used to promote businesses, organizations, brands, products, artists, bands, public figures, entertainment products, or social causes.

Fantastico: A system offered by most web hosts that is designed to make installing popular scripts, such as WordPress, Joomla, and osCommerce, extremely easy, usually requiring only one click of a button.

Feed Validator: A service that checks the syntax of Atom or RSS feeds to ensure that the code or language adheres to appropriate standards and guidelines.

Forum: An online community that gives users a way to communicate with one another and discuss general topics of interest.

Freelancer: A person who works independently for different companies at different times rather than being permanently employed by one.

FTP (file transfer protocol): A protocol used to transfer data between computers.

Google Analytics (www.google.com/analytics): A free web analytics solution that gives insight into website traffic, performance, and marketing effectiveness.

Googlebot: Google's spider program.

Google PageRank: A method used by Google to calculate the relevance and importance of a web page. The algorithm interprets a link from page A to page B as a vote by page A for page B, measuring both the quantity and quality of incoming links.

Graphic designer: A visual communicator who utilizes color, type, illustration, photography, and various print and layout techniques to create a design that communicates effectively and appeals to its intended audience.

Header tags: HTML tags that help draw attention to important information on a web page. Keywords contained in header tags can provide a rankings boost in search engine results.

Headline: A title that acts as the attention-getter for a story.

Home page: The initial front page of a website.

Hosted blog: URL that is usually a combination of the host site's name and a blogger's particular ID. For instance, at TypePad, a blogger's address would be bloggerID.typepad.com. Hosted blog sites can be found at TypePad.com, WordPress.com, and Blogger.com.

HTML (hypertext markup language): A computer programming language designed and used to create web pages.

Hyperlink: See *Clickable link.*

Inbound links: Incoming links to a website or web page.

Indexing: A data structure that allows information to be conveniently indexed to a database schema for efficient retrieval.

Index page: The initial front page of a website.

Interactive software: Programs with an interface that allows for human interaction, such as the ability to enter data or commands.

IP address (Internet Protocol address)**:** A unique numerical Internet Protocol address is assigned to and identifies every computer that connects to the Internet. IP addresses can be either static (where the assigned IP address never changes) or dynamic (where a new IP address is assigned every time a user connects to the Internet). An example of the format of an IP address is 213.742.39.33.

JavaScript: A simple programming language often used in conjunction with HTML or other web programming languages to make web pages more interactive.

Joomla: An open-source content management system used for publishing content to the Web.

Keyword: The specific word entered into a search engine by a user to search for information online.

Keyword density: The number of times (or ratio) a keyword is used on a particular web page.

Keyword phrase: The specific phrase entered into a search engine by a user to search for information online.

Keyword prominence: The location or placement of a keyword in the source code of a web document. The higher up on the page or tag a keyword is, the more weight it is given by a search engine.

Keyword proximity: The closeness between two or more keywords.

Keyword research: The process of determining the actual words and phrases people tend to use when searching for information online.

Keyword research tool: A tool that helps select the most appropriate and effective keywords for a website.

Keyword rich: When a web page is full of relevant keywords.

Keyword stuffing or spamming: The process of adding a superfluous number of keywords to a web page in such a way that the information ends up being nonsensical and user-unfriendly.

Landing page: The page of a website that a user lands on when arriving from an external source or link.

Layout: The way in which text and pictures are arranged on a page.

Length of session: A web statistic that shows the amount of time a visitor spent on a site.

Link: See *Clickable link.*

Link building: The process of actively cultivating incoming links to a site.

LinkedIn (www.linkedin.com)**:** A professional social networking site with over 85 million members worldwide.

Link popularity: A measure of the value of a site that is based on the number and quality of the sites that link to it.

Link text: See *Anchor text.*

Long tail keywords: Keyword phrases of three words or more that allow for a narrow and distinct search for information online.

Media kit: Book promotional tool that consists of information about a book, including details about its contents, intended audience, the author, and any related press clips.

Message board: An online community that gives users a way to communicate with one another and discuss general topics of interest.

Meta tags: Special HTML or XML tags (or coding statements) used by search engines to provide information about the contents of a web page.

Microblog: A simple Internet technology that allows a user to post short statements or sentences. Twitter (www.twitter.com) is an example of a microblogging service.

Multimedia: Multiple forms of media, such as text, graphics, and sound, that are integrated together.

Multipart MIME message: The combination of HTML and text in a single email message.

Navigational links: The internal links found on a website that provide users with a pathway between pages.

Navigation menu: The table of contents and links to the pages of a site.

News aggregator: A website or computer software that aggregates a specific type of information or news from multiple online sources.

Newsgroup: A place where people meet online to post ideas, ask questions, and comment on a particular topic or subject.

Newsletter: A periodic publication distributed digitally via email to an opt-in list of subscribers.

Niche market: A narrowly defined group of potential customers for a particular product or service.

Online community: A virtual community that consists of people who share common interests and use the Internet (websites, forums, chat rooms, email, etc.) to communicate, exchange, and collaborate online.

Opt-in: Where a user has consented to subscribe to, receive, and register for a newsletter by providing his or her email information.

Opt-out: Where a user has selected to unsubscribe from further email communications.

Orphan page: A web page that does not provide a way back to the originating page and forces a user to use the "Back" button of a browser.

osCommerce: E-commerce, online store–management software.

Outbound links: Links within a website that point to an external source or website.

Page count: The total number of pages in a book.

Page views: A statistic that shows the most popular pages viewed on a website.

PayPal (www.paypal.com)**:** An e-commerce business that allows payments and money transfers to be facilitated over the Web.

PDF (portable document format)**:** A proprietary digital file format created by Adobe that retains the formatting of a document regardless of platform used, whether Mac, Windows, or Unix.

Permalink (permanent link)**:** A URL that points to a specific blog post after it has passed from the front page into the archives.

Ping (for blogs)**:** The act of notifying blog search engines, directories, and other services of new and fresh content that appears on a blog site.

Plug-in: A software component that provides additional functionality or capabilities to a larger software application.

Podcast: A prerecorded audio or video file that can either be streamed or made available for download online and listened to or viewed on a personal computer or mobile device.

Podcatcher: An application that automatically checks for and downloads new podcasts via an RSS or XML feed.

PPC (pay per click)**:** A contextual advertisement model in which advertisers pay ad agencies (such as Google AdWords) whenever users click on their ads. AdWords is an example of PPC advertising.

Press release: A public announcement or statement prepared for distribution to various news media and online resources.

Press release distribution service: A free or paid service that distributes and syndicates a press release to an online audience that can consist of the media, news services, aggregators, search engines, bloggers, and others.

Psychographic information: The study and classification of people according to their attitudes, aspirations, values, beliefs, and other psychological criteria.

Publication: A book, magazine, newspaper, journal, or musical piece that is offered for sale.

Publisher: An individual or organization responsible for the production and dissemination of literature or information. Example duties include copyediting, graphic design, marketing, planning, and ad development.

Repeat visitors: A statistic that shows the number of visitors who return to a website more than one time.

Resource box: A brief bio that appears at the end of a published article that is used to promote a person, product, service, website, or blog.

RGB: The primary additive colors of red, green, and blue. When these colors are combined equally, they produce white; and when they are combined in different amounts, they can produce a broad array of colors. TV and computer monitors produce images using the RGB method.

Robot: Software that scans the Web with the purpose of indexing web pages for search engine results.

Robots.txt: A simple text file that tells a search engine not to crawl or index specified files or directories on a website.

Root directory: The first or topmost directory found on a website that includes all other directories.

Royalty-free music: Allows for the unlimited use of a musical piece or score in any medium as defined by the licensing agreement.

Royalty-free stock photography: Allows for the unlimited use of a photo in any medium as defined by the licensing agreement.

RSS (Really Simple Syndication or Rich Site Summary)**:** Allows you to syndicate or distribute content, or a summary of content, to subscribers who are automatically notified every time new content is added to your blog, website, or podcast series. The information is displayed through an RSS reader or news aggregator.

RSS feed: An XML document that displays content, or a summary of content, published from a website and presents this information in a standardized format.

RSS subscription: The process of subscribing to and receiving an RSS feed.

Screen reader: A talking browser for the visually impaired.

Search engine: A tool on the Internet that is used to search for and display relevant information.

Search engine friendly: Coding a web page in a way that makes it easily accessible and understandable to search engine spiders.

Search engine optimization (SEO)**:** The process of improving the visibility of a website or web page in search engine results according to a particular search term or phrase.

Search engine rankings: The position of a web page returned in search results when searched for with a specific keyword or keyword phrase.

SERP (search engine results page)**:** The results page that displays after a search or query, which consists of both paid and unpaid results.

Server: A computer designed to process requests and deliver data to other computers either over a local network or the Internet.

Short tail keywords: A one- or two-word search term, like "digital camera," that has a high search volume and is not very specific.

Social bookmark: A way to share users' bookmarks through a social media site such as StumbleUpon (www.stumbleupon.com).

Social media sharing buttons: Allow visitors to bookmark and share blog, website, podcast, or newsletter content with other users in their networks.

Social networking site: An interactive website that allows a user to set up an online profile, describe interests, post and share information, as well as connect and stay in touch with other users.

Spam email: Unsolicited email.

Spam triggers: Words or combinations of words, used in the subject line of emails that have been identified as the most commonly used by spammers for spam messages.

Spider: An automated software program that scans the Web with the purpose of storing and indexing web pages for search engine results.

Stand-alone blog: A blog that is hosted under its own unique domain name where the owner has full control over the design, features, and functionality.

Static web page: A web page that is delivered to the user exactly as stored and does not change its appearance, layout, or content in any way once displayed.

Stock photography: Ready-made images available for download online.

Streaming: Multimedia content that is sent over the Internet in real time.

Syndicated content: Content that appears on numerous websites throughout the Internet with the publisher's or writer's permission.

Tag: An HTML coding statement.

Tagging: Using particular keywords when describing articles, pictures, or posts.

Target market: A specific group of customers or market segment that a particular product or service is marketed to.

Text-based browser: A browser that displays web content minus any type of graphic element. Such browsers can be found on Unix and Linux systems.

Text link: Text on a web page that is usually underlined or highlighted, appears in blue, and is used as a clickable link, or hyperlink.

Trackback: An automated alert that is sent to a blog owner to let him or her know that one of his or her posts has been linked to or referenced from another site.

Twitter (www.twitter.com)**:** A microblogging platform in which users send out messages (or tweets) that consist of 140 characters or fewer.

TypePad (www.typepad.com)**:** Simple, no-fuss blogging solution that hosts a blog for a monthly fee. There are hundreds of themes and layouts available for customization.

Typography: The art or process of setting and arranging type on a page.

Unique visitors: This web statistic shows how many different people visit a website within a fixed time frame.

Unlimited domain hosting: A service offered by a select number of web hosts that allows you to host unlimited websites (using additional domain names) on a single hosting plan.

URL (Uniform Resource Locator)**:** The address of a web page on the Web.

URL shorteners: Services offered by companies such as Google (goo.gl) and bitly (bit.ly) that allow you to shorten lengthy URLs to make it easier for you share, tweet, or email them.

Vector image: A type of computer graphic created using mathematical formulas. Can be enlarged or reduced without any loss of quality.

Viral marketing: Word-of-mouth (sometimes known as word-of-mouse) marketing on the Internet.

Visitor path: A statistic that shows the actual path a visitor took while browsing a website.

Vlog: A video blog.

Web 2.0: Popular term for Internet technologies and applications that allow for a more social, collaborative, interactive, and responsive World Wide Web available to all regardless of technical ability. Includes social media, blogs, wikis, RSS, and social bookmarking sites.

Web-based template: A predesigned and formatted site design that can be personalized through the addition of text, images, or multimedia content.

Web designer: Responsible for the creation, design, layout, and coding of web pages.

Web host: A service or company that allows individuals and organizations to display websites that can be accessed over the Internet. Web hosts store HTML pages (and other types of code) on their servers.

Webinar: Short for "web-based seminar." A presentation, workshop, lecture, or seminar that is conducted online.

Webisode: A short audio or video presentation (episode) that appears on the Web.

Web maintenance agreement: An agreement by a web design company to allocate a specified number of hours that a site will be worked on in a specified period (week or month, etc.) for a certain fee.

Website: A collection of web pages or other digital assets that is relative to a common URL.

Website compatibility: Ensuring that a website displays and acts the same regardless of what browser, browser version, platform, or device it is being viewed on.

Web statistics: Information about the behavior of website visitors, providing graphical statistical data on things like what sites visitors came from, what search terms visitors used, what days and times they visited, and what paths they took through a site.

White hat SEO: Search engine optimization techniques and practices that are approved of by search engine companies.

White list: A list of email addresses or domain names that are allowed to pass through email-blocking programs or filters so messages can be received.

White paper: An authoritative report or guide that is often oriented toward a particular industry, issue, or problem.

WordPress: A web-based, open-source content management system (CMS) or blogging platform.

WordPress plug-ins: Tools or add-ons that extend WordPress's functionality.

World Wide Web Consortium (W3C)**:** The international standards organization for the World Wide Web.

XML (Extensible Markup Language)**:** A programming language specially designed to transport and store data.

YouTube (www.youtube.com)**:** A social media networking site designed for users to upload and share video content.

About the Author

Lorraine Phillips attended Jackson State University, where she acquired an MBA in business administration and a BS in computer science, graduating both programs with honors and distinction. She later went on to acquire an AA in graphic design from Bauder College and was elected to *Who's Who Among Students in American Colleges* for outstanding merit and accomplishments.

Lorraine is a creative information technology professional with over twelve years' experience in planning, developing, and publishing print and Internet projects. After a highly targeted Internet campaign, her first title, *Publish Your First Magazine*, became an Amazon Top 100 seller in its category; was rated 5 out of 5 (excellent) by *Writer's Digest*; and was selected as a Highlighted Title by *Independent Publisher*, which recognized and honored the book for exhibiting superior levels of creativity and originality as well as high standards of design and production quality.

Lorraine is CEO and founder of 360 Books. As a publishing consultant, she coaches and advises authors and publishers on the best practices for online book promotion, specializing in social media marketing, editorial, branding, and design. She is available for consultations, speaking engagements, presentations, lectures, and seminars anywhere you might be across the globe. For more, visit www.onlinebookbuzz.com.

Other Books by Lorraine Phillips

Publish Your First Magazine: A Practical Guide for Wannabe Publishers

Lorraine Phillips, former publisher of *SisterPower Magazine*, went directly from idea to newsstand after landing three distribution deals on her very first attempt and has now created a comprehensive, step-by-step guide that demonstrates her process and provides details on exactly how she did it. The book covers topics such as magazine business fundamentals, how to brand and design a publication, how to plan a magazine, business start-up costs, why a website is needed and what it should contain, how to work with printers, the importance of distribution, and the legalities of publishing. For more on *Publish Your First Magazine: A Practical Guide For Wannabe Publishers,* please visit www.publishyourfirstmagazine.com.

Your Personal Success Bible: 'The Secret' to Living the Life of Your Dreams!

Do you want more out of life? Have you not achieved some of the results you would like? Are you not doing the things you know you should? Or are you just not sure which direction to go next? Many of us are faced with the dilemma of trying to find the answers to these questions. We have been taught that success comes from 80 percent action and 20 percent thought, but this equation is wrong. True success comes from 80 percent thought and 20 percent action. Lorraine Phillips firmly believes there is nothing in life that cannot be modified or improved just by changing the way you think, and she provides simple, practical, effective techniques you can use in order to totally transform your life. For more, please visit www.yourpersonalsuccessbible.com.

Your Personal Success Quote Bible: Over 1,001 Inspirational Quotes for Daily Living!

This remarkable collection of insightful, uplifting, and profound words of wisdom will prove to be an invaluable tool for you on your journey to success. Created to keep you motivated and inspired you'll find quotes from Napoleon Hill, Socrates, Buddha, William Shakespeare, Tupac Shakur, Ralph Waldo Emerson, Lao Tzu, Albert Einstein, Robert Collier, Confucius, Bob Marley, Plato, and Deepak Chopra, to name a few. The book is divided into more than fifty relevant "daily living" categories and includes a complete index of authors, making the compilation a quick and easy, user-friendly guide in which you can always locate the perfect quote!

Index

A

B

C

D

E

F

G

H

I

K

L

R

S

T

U

V

W

Y

Z

CPSIA information can be obtained at www.ICGtesting.com
Printed in the USA
239133LV00002B/81/P
9 780982 276556